Crazy Cooks
and
Gold Miners

To Fred
With love
Christmas
1993

Jean

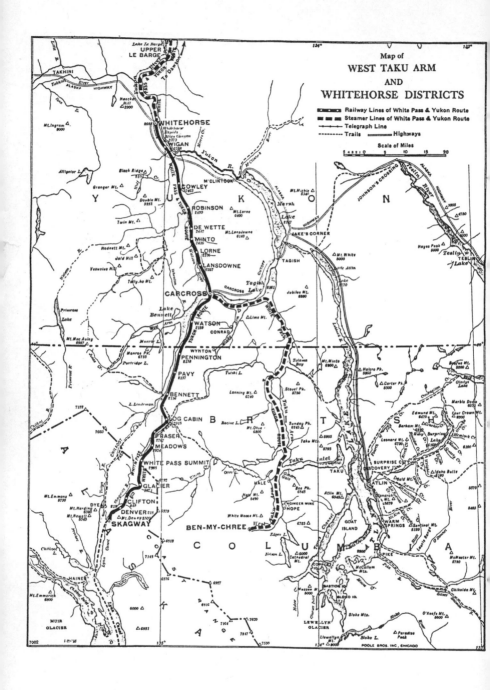

Map of

WEST TAKU ARM
AND
WHITEHORSE DISTRICTS

▄▄▄▄ Railway Lines of White Pass & Yukon Route
▄▄▄▄ Steamer Lines of White Pass & Yukon Route
┼┼┼┼ Telegraph Line
┈┈┈┈ Trails ═══ Highways

Scale of Miles

Crazy Cooks
and
Gold Miners

Joyce Yardley

ISBN 0-88839-294-X
Copyright © 1993 Joyce Yardley

Cataloging in Publication Data
Joyce Yardley, 1925-
   Crazy cooks and gold miners

ISBN 0-88839-294-X

1. Yardley, Joyce, 1925-   2. Yardley, Gordon.
3. Frontier and pioneer life—Yukon Territory.
4. Yukon Territory—Biography.   I. Title.
FC4023.1.Y37A3 1992   971.9'102'092
F1091.Y37 1992   C92-091782-8

Edited by: Herb Bryce
Production: Debbie Malyk and Lorna Lake

Front cover photos—clockwise:
   Left to right: Joe Jacquot, Gordon & Dave Small. Sitting: Dorothy
     Vill, Bob Vill & Joyce in 1968.
   A neighbors' gold in Atlin.
   Gordon with a pan full of gold.
Back cover photos:
   View of Lake Bennett from our house in Carcross.
   Joyce Yardley, 1992.

Published simultaneously in Canada and the United States by

HANCOCK HOUSE PUBLISHERS LTD.
19313 Zero Avenue, Surrey, B.C. V4P 1M7
(604) 538-1114   Fax (604) 538-2262

HANCOCK HOUSE PUBLISHERS
1431 Harrison Avenue, Blaine, WA 98231
(206) 354-6953   Fax (604) 538-2262

Contents

Acknowledgments

I would like to extend my sincere appreciation to the following people for their help and encouragement during the writing of this book: Cal Waddington, my son-in-law, for his most welcome contribution of the tape used in the Epilogue, and for his prompt and willing response in sending me pictures and slides; Roy Minter, who took the time out from his very busy schedule to read my manuscript—and to write his response to it in a generous foreword; my husband, Gordon, who gave me the computer to do the job, and without whom this book would never have been written; and my family and friends, who gave me loving support and forgave me for being preoccupied with memories so much of the time. Thank you, Richard Wright, for your helpful "workshop" at Duncan; and a special thanks to the publisher, David Hancock, and the editors, Herb Bryce and Lorna Lake.

Foreword

This book is a delight. It not only paints scene after scene of life in the Yukon, but it also reveals Joyce Yardley's love of adventure, and what it was like to be married at sixteen to Gordon Yardley, an engaging and thoroughly professional northern jack-of-all-trades. Together they ranched, fixed airplanes, logged, built and operated a northern lodge, and raised their kids. But these were just a few of their adventures—all of them loaded with challenge and excitement. Living in remote corners of the Yukon during the thirties, forties, and fifties was not easy. Not everything went right and when things went wrong there was not always help at hand. But you will not find a whimper nor a single word of regret on these pages; on the contrary, they are loaded with fun, thoughtful comment on life in Canada's Yukon, and, scattered throughout, are oases of rich dialogue covering everything from catching a crooked cook to hunting a marauding grizzly.

Joyce Yardley has recorded it all—and page by page reveals her adventures in the land of gold and the home of the Klondike. Her love of this land is obvious, and her ability to pluck the colorful details of her crowded life there makes her a notable northern scribe.

Crazy Cooks and Gold Miners reveals to us again and again that life is not really composed of great events, but rather it is a gathering of thousands of moments. Joyce Yardley reveals hers in a most entertaining way.

ROY MINTER
WHITEHORSE, YUKON

Introduction

I had wanted to write a book for years. What finally jolted me into action was a visit from a young couple from the Yukon. We had last seen them—oh, three years before, at least. Their little daughter was in kindergarten then. I wondered why they hadn't brought her along—and who in the world was the pretty girl in her early teens who came in the door with them?

"You remember Reagan, don't you?" her mother asked.

You guessed it—this was the same little girl! What had happened to those seven missing years? 'Can time possibly move that fast?' I asked myself, and concluded, 'I'm just going to have to run faster or I won't be able to keep up to it.'

That night I started my manuscript. It is a human-interest story about some of the experiences Gordon and I have had in the Yukon over our almost fifty years of marriage. My entrepreneurial husband has always preferred the independence of being self-employed to any other lifestyle, and that preference has led us down many unusual trails. Some of the people we've encountered along the way have made a deep impression in our minds and hearts—others have just amazed us with their strength, ingenuity, and humor.

Because our lives have been so entwined with the development of this fascinating land, it is almost impossible not to mention a few important historical events that have helped to shape the Yukon Territory and, in particular, the areas where most of this story took place.

Long before the Gold Rush in the Klondike, the only people living in the area around Dezadeash and Klukshu lakes were the native Indians, most of whom lived in the village of Nesketaheen, now known as Dalton Post, near the Tatsenshini River. Eventually these Indians began interacting and trading with the Indians of the West Coast, who came on foot from an area now known as

Haines, Alaska. These Chilkat Indians had already made contact with the white people, trading furs for guns, beads, coffee, and sugar, which in turn they carried inland to trade with the Stick Indians for caribou and moose skins, and for other types of fur. Both tribes traveled back and forth over the well-worn trail for many years.

The first white men to arrive in that area were Jack Dalton and his partner, and the trail became known as the Dalton Trail. Then, in 1898, gold was discovered in the Dawson area and a huge stampede of miners, speculators, businessmen, "ladies of the night," and missionaries swarmed into the relatively unheard of Yukon Territory by the tens of thousands.

From Haines, they traveled on foot or with donkeys and horses over the Dalton Trail, and on to connect with the increasingly crowded Dawson Trail.

Many more climbed the Chilkoot and White passes between Skagway, Alaska, and Lake Bennett. The shores of Lake Bennett became a crowded, frantic beehive of activity, with thousands of boats being built and sold for use on the remainder of the trip to Dawson City. From there, the gold seekers traveled over lakes and rivers, in the winter by horse-drawn sleds; and they traveled over the "Tram Lines" that hauled sleds, wagons, and people on wooden rails around Miles Canyon, south of Whitehorse.

The next giant step in the development of the Yukon must be accredited to the founders of the White Pass and Yukon Route, and to the engineers and organizers who have contributed to the strong and steady growth of the many branches of that company right up to the present time. The railway was a brilliant feat of engineering, accomplished in spite of gigantic difficulties and obstacles encountered along the treacherous route.

The White Pass Company has been the backbone of the Yukon since 1898. Based in Whitehorse, it has been the one most significant and important factor in the early development of the Territory, providing Yukoners with employment—as well as their first real link to the outside world. Their navigation branch, British Yukon Navigation, supplied transportation and freight to the mines and communities along the Yukon River via a large fleet of colorful sternwheel riverboats. One of these "paddle wheelers" was the S.S. *Tutshi*, which was used on Tagish Lake, and based in Carcross, Yukon. The last of these boats was retired in 1955.

The "shipyard" in Whitehorse was also owned and operated by the White Pass. It was located at the north end of the railroad tracks, consisted of warehouses and maintenance shops, and created another source of summer employment for mechanics, blacksmiths, and carpenters; and, in the winter months, it was the White Pass that hired men to run the horse-drawn sleds between Whitehorse and Dawson City over the old Dawson Trail.

It was against this backdrop that I arrived in the world on November 3, 1925, in the Whitehorse General Hospital, increasing the winter population of that town by one, for a total of 251 people.

White Pass Airways flew between Skagway and Whitehorse, Mayo and Dawson City from its own flight strips, using a variety of aircraft, including bush planes equipped with skis and floats, and one of the largest passenger-carrying planes in Canada, the Condor biplane.

This company was sold in the early 1940s and eventually became part of Canadian Pacific Airways.

Then, in the spring of 1942, came another colossal milestone in the history of the Yukon Territory—the construction of a military tote road, 1,520 miles in length. The Alcan Highway, as it was called in those days, was completed in just nine months for the purpose of transporting army personnel and supplies to Alaska during the war years. It was a joint venture between the Canadian and United States governments.

The railroad and trains were leased to the U.S. Army for the duration of the war.

The White Pass eventually went on, in the 1950s, to introduce the "container" method of transporting freight, a technique that was soon used all over the world. They designed and built their own ships to haul these containers between Vancouver, British Columbia, and Skagway, Alaska, creating an integrated transportation system of ships, trains, and trucks from Vancouver to Dawson City—and a petroleum distribution and storage plant based in Whitehorse.

Looking back now, in 1992, it seems a bit incredible (and wonderful in a way) that so much water has passed under the bridge...yet here we are, the whole family still doing business with the same White Pass company that provided the Yukon with its lifeline to the rest of the world—so long ago, in 1898.

And we are also thankful that we have had the privilege of becoming close friends with an old Indian man by the name of Jimmy Kane, who actually remembered...and shared with us his reactions to the first white man he had ever seen, Jack Dalton.

1

Dating in Wartime Whitehorse

"Don't be ridiculous! You want to get married? At sixteen? There'll be plenty of time for that when you're finished high school."

"Mother, we've made up our minds."

"What's all the hurry?" Dad broke in. "Wait a while and see if you still feel the same way in another month or two."

"I can't wait," I wailed. "You don't know these girls in town. They can't keep their hands off him."

"There are 10,000 soldiers in Whitehorse now. Surely they can find a boyfriend somewhere!"

For a fleeting second I thought a little wistfully about all the possibilities out there, but quickly rallied. I sensed an angle here that could possibly be used in this argument with my parents.

Emphatically I exclaimed, "That's another thing! With that many men roaming the streets, it probably won't be safe for a single girl to go out of the house anymore. At least I'd have someone to look after me."

My father looked thoughtful. My mother, suspecting that he was wavering, stormed into the kitchen. Dad and I looked at each other; his expression was sad and I knew that he was thinking.

"It's going to be so quiet around here with the last one leaving home."

I reached up and gave him a hug.

"It'll be all right, Daddy," I whispered. "It's not like we're going away or anything."

"I'll see if I can persuade your mother," he said. "But he'd better be good to you!"

I had met Gordon in the fall of 1941, on the narrow gauge White Pass and Yukon Route railway. Our Whitehorse high school basketball team had just beaten the pants off our neighboring town of Skagway, Alaska, and we were all in high spirits on our way home.

When we got to the Carcross station, the train stopped to let on six men. They rode in the passenger car with us, causing a flurry of interest among the girls of the team. Strangers were coming to our town! This was still a novelty in Whitehorse, where everyone knew each other.

One of them turned out to be Gordon, the man I would be spending the rest of my life with. Every time I glanced his way our eyes would meet, and I'd turn away in embarrassment—caught red-handed. After a while, he came and sat beside me and we started talking. I could feel the envious glances of my teammates without even looking at them.

Gordon had been working as a deckhand on a paddle wheeler in Carcross, but was now on his way to Whitehorse to take a job as mechanic for Pan American Airlines.

"Do you think we should take in a movie tonight?" he asked me.

"Sounds okay to me," I answered.

It was the understatement of the year. After the movie we went to the "Cabaret" in the Whitehorse Inn, where all the kids in town used to congregate, and we danced to the jukebox and drank coke. Later, he walked me home.

'Wonder if he'll try to kiss me?' I thought. He didn't.

Then I worried, 'I'm not sure whether that's a good sign or not.'

The next time Gordon and I went out, it was to dinner at a restaurant. He called for me at home. Suddenly, there he was, standing in the doorway, impeccably dressed, good looking, and — gulp—twenty-four years old! Just as suddenly, my knees turned to water; fear stabbed me in the stomach—and I just knew I was dressed all wrong. My glasses were probably crooked, I looked like a child, and...I had never been to dinner before with a man. Skating, yes; movies, yes. But this was *formal.* All my insecurities hit me like a ton of bricks. I restrained myself from rushing to my room and changing into something more sophisticated. I stammered something stupid to my folks.

"Don't wait up for me."

I hoped it would sound worldly. I walked out the door, red-faced but with my head held high.

When we reached the cafe we ran into Gordon's friend, Si McLeod, and I suggested we invite him to join us, which he did. It saved the day for me, as he and Gordon became engrossed in man talk. They didn't notice me trying valiantly to swallow the food past the nervous lump in my throat. Finally sanity returned, and I began to enjoy myself as the two of them vied for my attention by teasing me unmercifully. By the time Gordon walked me home, I was on cloud nine again, and felt like a queen.

Gordon was now working night shift, from midnight to 8:00 A.M. The next morning on my way to school, I ran into him by coincidence as he was leaving work. We stood and chatted for what seemed like five minutes but must have been longer as I was ten minutes late for school. I had to stay in that day and write "I must not be late for school" on the board one hundred times. This I did cheerfully—it had been worth it.

Strangely enough, the same coincidence occurred every morning when I was on my way to school. One day my teacher, Laurie Todd, looked at me sadly and said, "Joyce, I'm not going to ask you to be on time again, as it's no use. I give up. You win." With a shock, I realized he thought I was doing this as an act of defiance, which was not so—in fact, I was very fond of our red-headed teacher. I was never late for school again.

In November I turned sixteen. Gordon and I began seeing more of each other. On December 7, Pearl Harbor was bombed by the Japanese, and talk of a road to the Arctic for transporting army personnel and weapons was being discussed. It wasn't until February, 1942, though, that the U.S. Army issued the directive to build a military road to Alaska.

The arrival of the troops had quite an impact on our little town. In just four weeks, we went from 300 people to 3,000. Then they just kept arriving and we lost track of the numbers. We did know, however, that 20,000 men were employed in the construction of the highway.

Things were happening so fast it made my head swim. Our lifestyle had been drastically disrupted. One minute I'd be caught up in the excitement of it all, and the next I'd be longing for something permanent and safe. With all the changes taking place so swiftly, and being in love to boot, school seemed to me to be irrelevant and unimportant.

When Gordon suggested we get married, I couldn't have agreed more. Luckily, my parents thought he was quite nice. He'd do thoughtful things like taking my skis home with him and bringing them back all waxed and polished. He helped Dad split firewood, and even joined us for church once or twice. (I tease him about this now, almost half a century later, as he's never been to church since, except for weddings and funerals.)

It still came as a shock to Mom and Dad when I broke the news about wanting to get married. Mother finally came around to Daddy's way of thinking. She still stipulated that I should get to know the value of money, by earning my own living for a while (never dreaming that I would do it) before getting married.

Whitehorse was now swarming with U.S. Army men in uniform. The White Pass trains were groaning with heavy loads of supplies of all descriptions, and were running around the clock. Other supplies were being flown in, and construction began on the airport to accommodate the sudden escalation of air traffic.

A tent city sprang up overnight, followed by shipments of quonset hut sections. Soon there were rows of army barracks and quonset huts, complete with spotlights on poles lining the walkways between them.

The first trainload of supplies into town was firewood. There was ample firewood growing all over the Yukon, but the army must have believed the north was all tundra, ice, and snow.

The community hall was filled to the ceiling with canned goods before warehouses could be built to hold them. Unfortunately, the hall caught fire one day. As the first wall collapsed, cases of food spilled out onto the ground. Later they were piled twenty feet high on the vacant lot left by the fire. Many toppled into the street, where trucks and army jeeps ran right over them. The odd looter would come out after dark with a dog sleigh and haul a load home. When the freezing weather came, there was still no place to store these canned goods, and by spring the wet snow had made the cardboard crates soggy and weak. Finally, the army hauled them all to the dump.

The waste in those times was unbelievable. It is strange that just a short time before that we had been hearing about shortages and rationing "outside," and much talk about the terrible depression. Yet, suddenly, there was this incredible waste of food.

The only thing I can remember being rationed in Whitehorse was liquor. My parents lived just across the road from the old liquor store and we could watch the long queues of people waiting to buy their rations; some who had never had a drink in their lives were getting theirs for friends or to sell.

One day Mom was preparing dinner for some guests and discovered she was out of vinegar for a salad dressing, so Dad offered to walk to the store and get some for her. He was on his way back home with his parcel when a man walked up alongside him, grabbed the bag with the vinegar bottle out of Dad's hand, stuck a twenty-dollar bill in his pocket, and ran like hell.

Imagine that man's chagrin when he opened the paper bag later.

Larry Higgins was the liquor vendor and government agent in town. Single-handedly he ran the liquor store, sold vehicle, fishing, and hunting licenses, and even acted as justice of the peace and game commissioner. In the summertime, he was assigned a helper by the name of Carl Bryden, and during the long lineups on paydays he had an extra man. I often wonder how many hundreds of government employees it takes now to handle the work that Larry Higgins used to do.

All the stores and businesses in town were sold out of stock within the first few days of the soldiers' arrival. It must have been slim pickings for the merchants at first, because supplies had to be shipped by boat from Vancouver to Skagway, and then by train to Whitehorse. The Army had priorities on all shipments, and although the boys were fed in their own mess halls, with everything supplied, they still bought out the stores.

These being wartime years, my brother Ted volunteered for active duty in the Royal Canadian Air Force. His wife, Dolly, and two-year-old daughter, Sharon, waited for him in Whitehorse. Ted never returned from his last mission as air gunner over Germany. He was reported missing. So, suddenly, we became acutely conscious of the tragedy and horror of war. I don't think

16

my mother ever stopped hoping, even after March 14, 1945, when it was confirmed that he had been shot down.

A mountain peak in the Canyon Creek area of the Alaska Highway was later named Mount Richards in honor of my brother Ted. I had loved him dearly, and he left a void in my life—in the lives of everyone in the family—that could never be filled.

It was around this time that Gordon purchased a car—one of the six in town, if I remember correctly. Most of the vehicles in Whitehorse then were pickups and, mostly, working vehicles such as wood and water delivery trucks. His was a La Salle (a small Cadillac) and a very classy-looking model. We would go for drives to the "Beam Station" and back (that was where the Air Force sent out security signals to incoming aircraft). The station was five miles out of town and was serviced by the only road fit for a car at the time.

To prove my maturity to mother, I went to talk to Isaac Taylor of Taylor and Drury Co. Ltd. and asked him for a job. T & D's, as we called the company, had general stores and trading posts throughout the Yukon, with posts at Pelly, Ross River, Champagne, Sheldon Lake, Teslin, and Carmacks. Some of these were as far as 500 miles from any transportation, other than bush planes and dog teams in the winter months. T & D had been trading with the Indians since the turn of the century. The company flew supplies in to these posts and took furs back out. The ones located on the river could be serviced by boat, and the company had two of their own small paddle wheelers for that purpose. The main store was in Whitehorse, where my father managed the dry goods department.

I had no problem obtaining employment. They needed all the help they could get. Now I had the excuse I needed to quit school and become engaged. I started in the grocery department—my first job!

An old family friend, Charlie Atherton, worked there too. His support made my first days much easier. The other clerk in our grocery department was George Aylwin. Forty-five years later, he still lived in Whitehorse and whenever I'd meet him on the street, he would tease me about getting a job at sixteen—just to prove I was old enough to be married.

17

One day a young lady came into the store and started a conversation while I helped her pick out her groceries. I was struck by how beautiful her face looked; she seemed to be glowing with happiness.

"I hear you're making plans for your wedding," she said. "Is it true?"

"Yes, it is."

"Good for you. I hope you'll be as happy as Les and I are. There's nothing in the world like it!"

She was so warm and friendly that I felt cheerful for the rest of the day. It turned out that she was the wife of Les Cook. He was a bush pilot with a reputation for being an excellent pilot, though everyone considered him too daring in the chances he took.

A short time after that, I was walking home from work when a plane took off from the airport, circled over town, then suddenly lost altitude and fell from the sky—crashing on the street in front of Isaac Taylor's house.

Apparently Les's wife was among the pedestrians downtown who went rushing to the scene. Les died right there—along with two mechanics who were with him.

For Better—For Worse

Gordon, at this time, was renting a neat little log cabin with his friend and coworker, Jimmy Patterson. It belonged to the Cyr family, and it was close to the clay bluff that rims the west side of town and rises to the plateau where the airport is. Whitehorse spreads out between this bluff and the Yukon River on the east side.

We set the wedding date for July 24. Jimmy (or Jock, as everyone calls him now), like the good friend he was, began looking for another place to live.

We were married in the Old Log Church by Reverend Peter Chapel on July 24, 1942. My bouquet was from my mother's garden—sweet peas and baby's breath. Jimmy Patterson was our best man, Phyllis Walker (now Hinds) was my bridesmaid, and my sister, Wilda, was matron of honor.

I moved through the ceremony and reception as if in a dream, making the correct responses, but having no sense of reality. It was as if I were watching someone else...walking down the aisle on my father's arm...going through the traditional ceremony. Even now, thinking back to that day, it still seems like a dream. The reception was a blur of people and faces, of saying polite things, and wishing it were over so we could leave and start our new life together.

Not until we were driving away in our shiny black La Salle—with all the decorations and tin cans tied to it—did the dreamlike, floating sensation start to dissipate and, mercifully, reality returned. We drove out to my parents' weekend cabin at Ice Lake, three miles from town, where the silence was broken only by the calling of the loons.

The next day we temporarily traded cars with Joe Morrison, Gordon's boss with Pan American Airways, as ours was a bit low for the drive to Carcross. Besides, Joe coveted the La Salle like crazy, so we knew he wouldn't mind.

Arriving in Carcross, we boarded the good ship *Lou Anne*, piloted by Captain Jones, with George Rose as engineer, and set out for Atlin, British Columbia, on our honeymoon.

By nightfall, we landed at Taku Arm, where we slept in a double sleeping bag on the wooden floor of the little train station, which I thought we had all to ourselves. Wrong! To our surprise and chagrin, some other folks arrived late in their small boats and spread out their bedding alongside us. It wasn't easy the next morning—struggling to dress unobtrusively inside that sleeping bag.

A few hours later, we were riding the shortest registered railroad in the world to Scotia Bay. Ted Smyth picked us up in his boat and took us across Atlin Lake to the small mining town of Atlin. The sun turned the wake's white froth into a silver spray and the reflection of the rugged beauty of the snow-capped mountains took my breath away. We pulled up to the public wharf, gathered up our belongings, and said good-bye to Ted.

The town is well nicknamed "Switzerland of the North." Of course, I've not been to Switzerland yet, but I can't help thinking that, maybe, Atlin might even have a little edge on it.

It was my first visit to this part of the country. So far, everything, even the weather, seemed to be conspiring to make this the best honeymoon anyone could wish for. Gordon already knew most of the townsfolk, having visited there before we met, and I'm sure half of them were on the street that day. By the time each of them had stopped to visit, I was getting hungry and tired. A shy person by nature, I was still quite nervous meeting strangers. In Whitehorse, we rarely met three or four new people a year. That day, in Atlin, I had already been introduced to a dozen or more.

We checked in the at the old Kootenay Hotel. I did my best to appear nonchalant, and to ignore the inquisitive stares of the people in the lobby. They all seemed to be sizing up Gordon's young bride fairly closely. 'Hope they're not all going to the dining room,' I thought. My wish was not granted. After we'd finished dinner and climbed the stairs to our room, a happy feeling of relief flooded over me as I ran water into the tub. Finally we were going to have some time together alone. When I emerged from the bathroom, all rosy and glowing, Gordon was still dressed, even to his shoes.

"Aren't you going to relax for a while?" I asked as I bounced up on the bed.

"Oh, I thought we'd go down and have a beer with the gang."

"Can't we do that tomorrow, instead?"

"Well, they're probably expecting us tonight. They get tired of each other's company in a small town like this."

"Big deal! It sounds like you're tired of mine already."

"Don't be silly. You're just being stubborn," he said. "We don't have to stay very long."

"Just go on down without me, then. I've had enough visiting for one day."

'What if he really does go?' I was thinking. 'Oh, he would never do that—would he?' Guess I wasn't a very good judge of human nature at that age. He would rather have died than give in right then; it would have been setting a precedent. But my stubbornness matched his perfectly. When he realized he wasn't getting anywhere trying to talk me into going with him, he turned and started to go out the door.

"I shouldn't be too long."

"Take your time," I retorted.

When the door closed behind him, I collapsed in a flood of tears. My heart was broken. This was the end of our marriage. Everything was over. My whole world had come crashing down over my head. Finished. I cried myself to sleep.

It must have been a couple of hours later when I awoke to find Gordon sliding into bed beside me. Relief flooded over me.

"Hi there, little one," he said. "Got over your mad yet?"

I guess I had. I flicked the light off so he couldn't see my swollen eyes, then slipped into his arms and held on tight. "Just try to get away from me again," I said. I don't remember for sure, but I don't think we went downstairs until noon the next day.

Gordon had taken only a week off from work, so it wasn't long before we were back again in Whitehorse.

At home, I tackled the very new experience of being a housewife. I'd never done laundry (it was a wooden scrub board and galvanized tub at that time) or cooked meals before. By the time our first married Christmas rolled around, I felt experienced enough to stuff a turkey. To show off my cooking expertise, I invited Mom and Dad to dinner. It turned out to be a success.

Gordon told his favorite story about my first attempt to make bread. (I must warn you that a few of his stories are not 100 percent true. Ninety-nine and a half percent maybe—but the odd time he will get a bit carried away.) With Mom's bread recipe in hand, surely it would be a snap. I got out the flour, the big bowl, rolled up my sleeves, and pitched in. The more I kneaded, the stickier the big mass of dough got. I added more and more flour, until, finally, it felt right. I sat down with a book and waited for it to rise...and waited...and waited. Nothing was happening. It looked like a big heavy blob just sitting there—not moving an inch! Gordon was due home in an hour, and to avoid embarrassment, I decided to get rid of it. But how? If I put it in the slop pail (there was no plumbing in the cabin), he would notice when he carried it out. Putting all that dough in the wood stove would certainly put the fire out. I wandered over to the window and stood there looking out, trying to formulate a plan. My eyes focused on the end of the yard where the gophers had dug many holes. Wheels started turning in my head. Then I whirled around. 'Quickly,' I thought, 'before he gets home.' I grabbed the bowl, a butcher knife, and tucked the broom under my arm.

Working fast, I cut off lumps of dough, stuffed them into the gopher holes, and tamped them in with the broom handle. 'Mission accomplished; and just in time,' I thought. However, it was an hour or so later before Gordon arrived so I needn't have rushed.

"Did you know you have big mushrooms growing in the yard?" he asked.

"Mushrooms!" I responded, and rushed to the window to see.

Sure enough, in each gopher hole, warmed by the sun and rising beautifully, was a big, perfectly round mushroom. *Bread* mushrooms!

Before I could stop him, he was out there to gather them for dinner. I flung myself red-faced on the bed. In a minute or two, he was back.

Trying to keep a straight face, he said, "Guess there won't be enough for dinner. Soon as I touch them they shrink away to nothing."

This is just one of many stories I have to put up with when he entertains our friends.

The Pole Contract

Toward the end of March, 1943, Gordon heard of a contract that was coming up for bid, to install a telephone pole line for the U.S. Army. It was to run from Skagway to Whitehorse, and from Carcross east to Jake's Corner on the Alaska Highway.

"I wonder if I should put a bid in?" he asked.

He was really just thinking out loud. By this time I had discovered that Gordon wasn't easily influenced by my opinion, but at least he made the gesture. A good habit, I thought.

"Of course you should," I told him. "Maybe we'll make enough money to buy our own house."

"It'll mean moving to Carcross."

"That would be fun; a change of scene," I replied, getting into the spirit. He put in the bid that afternoon. Impatiently, we waited for the verdict. The news finally arrived: we had been awarded the contract.

Gordon gave up his job as mechanic for Pan American, traded vehicles again with his now ex-boss, Joe Morrison, and we moved to Carcross.

At that time it was impossible to find a place to live. The road to Carcross was being built by black soldiers from the 95th Engineering Regiment of the U.S. Army. Actually, about a third of the men working on the Alcan Highway were black soldiers. All the houses and log cabins were taken, even though there were the usual rows of quonset huts on the edge of town.

We finally had to pitch a couple of tents—one for sleeping and one for cooking. I had always enjoyed camping—but it felt different when you had a home to return to when the camping trip was over.

The sleeping tent was okay. We had an airtight heater which kept us warm during the night. However, the canvas on the cook tent was khaki colored and got stifling hot from the April sun beating down, plus the heat from the cookstove. I remember dripping with perspiration when cooking and heating water in that makeshift kitchen.

'And this is what was going to be so much fun,' I thought.

I was glad when an old prospector—Skelly, he was called—decided it was time for his summer prospecting trip into the hills. We talked him into renting his cabin to us. The cabin wasn't much more than walls, a bed, a table, and a cookstove. It had an attic, a kind of loft really, with a ladder leading up to it. After living in the tents, though, it was a real improvement.

Gordon was busy gathering a crew for falling poles. Most of the men he hired were Natives from Carcross. He paid them a dollar a pole. They could each fall twenty-five to thirty a day, which meant good money as the going wage was less than ten dollars a day.

The problem was that after a few days they'd feel rich and would want to take time off. They would invent all kinds of excuses—from needing to get a moose to having to go into White-horse to see the dentist—as all that money was burning a hole in their pockets and needed to be spent.

23

Gordon would get really frustrated. I tried to cheer him up with home baking, but too often it had the opposite effect. The oven in the old wood-burning stove had rust holes in it. Some of the mouth-watering treats I had planned turned out to be more like lumps of clay.

'I'll knit him an Indian sweater, instead,' I decided.

Gordon gave all the men a raise, to try to keep them around. Now they were getting a dollar fifty a pole. This meant that they got richer faster, so they took time off from work sooner and more often.

Then he got word that there were men available from British Columbia at Telegraph Creek. So Gordon got Herman Peterson to fly in some of these Natives to add to his crew. They were tall men—strong and hardy. Gordon was impressed by their willingness and apparent ability to do the job well.

Finally, he had his crew organized. Before going out to wood camp, though, they congregated in Matthew Watson's General Store to pick up last-minute odds and ends.

The train station in Carcross is only fifty yards from the store as the tracks run right through the center of town. A train was pulling in at the time. The whistle from the steam engine blew and suddenly the store was vacated.

Matthew looked up, perplexed because their work gloves, chocolate bars, and other purchases were still lying on the counter.

He looked at Gordon. "Where did they go?"

Then both grinned as they realized that the men had never seen or heard a train before.

It was the first time out of Telegraph for most of them, and they weren't going to miss the event.

In those days there was no road into Telegraph Creek. Travel was confined to small bush planes and boats down the Stikine River and on out to the coast. So the tree-falling began.

Before long, I realized that next December there was going to be a small addition to our family, and suddenly the future took on a new meaning. This was the most important thing that had happened in our lives so far. To me it was a miraculous revelation—as if this had never happened to anyone else before; I was responsible for a new life growing inside me! It was exciting,

24

scary, and my first real lesson in patience. I was forced to resign myself to eight more months of anticipation.

Gordon was almost as excited as I was, although he tried to appear very nonchalant about the whole thing. I was beginning to see through his reserved exterior.

With the job under way and in control, Gordon began to arrange for better living quarters. There was a Royal Canadian Mounted Policeman named Blatta living on Tagish Lake a couple of miles from Carcross, at a place still called Blatta's Point. He and his wife raised mink and fox as a sideline, as did quite a few others up and down the lake. Blatta was being transferred to another post at the time, and had sold his animals, and now the large pale gray lumber house was for sale. There was no road to their place. They traveled by boat or foot during the summer or used snowshoes and a dog team in the winter. In spite of this inconvenience, we liked the house. It was in good shape and had lots of room inside. We bought it and moved in, with the intention of moving it to Carcross as soon as possible.

The event I remember most at Blatta's Point happened on a cold but sunny day in mid-April. Snow was still on the ground, and we hadn't yet shoveled the trail to the outhouse. There was a good crust on the snow, as it had been melting during the days and freezing again at night. I made it to the "little house" all right, but coming back I stepped on a soft spot which couldn't hold my weight. I was wearing a dress and bedroom slippers at the time. Down I went, standing there with my legs in two deep holes in the snow. When I tried to move, the ragged edges of the ice cut into my bare flesh and hurt like the dickens. I had to stand there and yell for Gordon. It seemed to take ages before he heard me. Finally, he glanced out the window and saw me stranded there in tears. He came and rescued me, trying to keep a straight face while carrying me into the house.

We enjoyed living there, except that Gordon had to be away a lot. It became too isolated for me as my pregnancy progressed. So we rented a house in Carcross across the river from Johnny Johns, an Indian outfitter and big game guide. Johnny had a reputation for being a character and was well-known for his antics and storytelling eloquence. Being quite a philosopher and

25

aided by the old "Demon Rum," he could entertain his hunters or a bar full of friends for hours with his poems and stories, which he loved to tell in his gravelly voice.

When Gordon had time to spare, we went to Blatta's Point to work on the house—putting skids underneath so we could move it to town over the ice. When the time came, however, our little Cat (Caterpillar tractor) just sputtered and gave up under the weight, shortly after we had reached the lake. Now we were faced with a dilemma. Should we wait until next summer and make it into a raft, or tear it down now, haul the lumber to town, and start building a new house? Eventually, we chose the last plan.

Our work was definitely cut out for us now—finishing the pole contract and a new home as well. The pole contract turned out to be lucrative. An old single-pole line already existed, but the poles were rotted out. Gordon had to supply new peeled poles, put cross poles on, then deliver them to the post holes into which they would be set.

They started cutting about twenty miles down the lake from Carcross, where there was an excellent stand of suitable timber. Gordon had bought an old two-ton Holt Caterpillar, with a cross bar on it (instead of levers) for steering. The next purchase was a three-ton Chevrolet truck with a sixteen-foot deck to haul poles over the frozen lake into town. Shortly after that, the U.S. Army issued Gordon a 6 x 6 truck (six wheels, two in the front and four in the back, all driving) to use as well.

The condition of the ice that spring was not the best. All the snowdrifts on the lake had started to melt, forming water on the ice. When going across Windy Arm with the trucks, the men had about fifteen inches of water to drive through. They couldn't see the ice at all for six or seven miles and it looked like they were driving in the lake itself. This was all right, however, as at that stage the ice was still solid and safe for travel.

As time went on, the water all disappeared through the ice, which became dry once more and light blue in color; that meant it had started to "honeycomb" from the bottom up, but would still be safe for a while yet. When it began to turn dark and wet again, though, the time had definitely come to stop traveling on it.

The ice began to disintegrate first, right along the shoreline, which made it hard to get the truck and its load on and off the lake. A creek which flowed into the lake had formed a mini-glacier by freezing, then partially thawing and flooding over by day and freezing again at night. This created a small ice bridge to travel across.

The snow in town, and in much of the countryside, had gone by the beginning of May. Then one night there was a late snowfall; it was just a skiff, really, but enough to turn the ground white again. The following morning, Ernie Butterfield came along just as Gordon was leaving for work.

"How about catching a ride with you?" he asked. "I'm going back to the ranch and it'll save me hiking a few miles."

"Sure, hop in," Gordon told him.

When they arrived at the ice bridge, Gordon didn't think it looked very solid.

"Looks safe enough to me," said Ernie.

Gordon realized that the man was an experienced ice traveler—with a team and sleigh; but that was a lot different from a truck with heavy dual wheels. He wasn't too happy about it, but they decided to give it a try anyway. The front wheels of the truck held up all right, but the rear ones started sinking and cracking up the ice. It was too late to holler whoa now—so Gordon poured the coal to it, and with a great roar the truck just managed to make it out to the solid ice. Looking back, they saw the cracked ice behind them had turned into a gaping, open water hole.

Later that morning, another fellow came by with the intention of taking his truck out to the wood lot to pick up some wood for his furnace. He saw Gordon's truck tracks standing out clearly in the snow—coming to a halt at the water's edge—then continuing on the ice over the lake.

'Well,' he thought, 'I guess if those guys made it okay, I can do likewise.'

He gunned his motor and made a run for it. Instead of lifting up onto the ice as he'd planned, the truck just sank down and kept on going down—until the water was up to the hood. The man had to crawl out the window and go back into town to get someone to pull his truck back out.

Gordon figured he could keep hauling poles for a while longer by using the old Cat and putting the load on a couple of sleighs. This distributed the weight of the logs over a larger surface.

Twelve miles from town, underground springs bubbled up through the ice and formed large holes at the shallowest part of the lake. These could reach ten feet in diameter and were scattered over the ice for four or five miles. The drivers had to work their way between them as best as they could. Gordon started riding on the front sleigh to steer the Cat from there by tying two ropes onto the cross bar, as if he were driving a horse. Apparently if a Caterpillar falls through the ice, it goes over backward and there's little chance of jumping clear. This method was safer— after a fashion. As they passed between the holes, the weight of the load would cause the water to boil out and over the ice like a fountain, and when they had gone on by, the ice would rise again and the water would rush back down with a loud sucking noise.

What a lucky thing I never knew what was happening until it was all over. I'm afraid my peace of mind would have been damaged permanently. In later years, I came to understand ice travel well but then I knew little about conditions that late in the season. Every night when Gordon came home for dinner, I would question him about his day.

"Oh, everything's coming along fine," he'd say. "Same old grind."

2

A Tragic Weekend

The reconstruction work on the Blatta house was going well. We were building in Carcross on Lake Bennett's waterfront and had a view that couldn't be surpassed. Situated at the end of a long row of log houses in the west end of town, it was a wonderful location. The beach was two miles of soft, clean, white sand and, if the bench covered with shallow lake water was included, the beach was a quarter-mile wide. It gradually merged into undulating sand dunes that swept up from the lake and stretched for another two miles toward the Watson River.

There were about a hundred residents in Carcross at the time. In a sense, we were all neighbors. Going to town meant Whitehorse, fifty miles away. We were still living in Johnny's house.

On October 16, 1943, Gordon finished his breakfast, kissed me good-bye, and went off to work on our new house. He was putting on some roofing when he looked up and saw a plane flying low over the lake.

He could tell that the aircraft was in trouble; but even as he watched, it suddenly dropped right out of the sky and into the water. He saw men scrambling out into the lake, and the plane starting to sink. In a second, Gordon was off that roof and running down the beach to get his boat. He met George Simmons, coming from his house, and they flung themselves into the boat and shoved off.

"My God, George, are we going to make it on time?"

"I sure as hell hope so," George replied.

Later we found out what had happened.

A couple of officers with the U.S. Air Force had decided to test a Flying Fortress, one of the new four-engined Boeing B-17-Gs, which had just undergone some repairs in Whitehorse. They were going to take it to Juneau, Alaska. Fifteen other fellows went along for the ride. They did not know that someone had forgotten to hook up the de-icers on the carburetors.

The weather in Whitehorse was mild at takeoff but when they got into the colder weather over the Coast Range, they realized that something was wrong and attempted to land on the Carcross airstrip.

Apparently the pilot shut off his remaining two motors too soon after the first two froze up, and the plane dropped forty to fifty feet to the water, breaking the fuselage. This let water into the plane and caused it to sink right away. If the pilot had feathered the props when the motors died, he could have held enough altitude to make it to the airfield.

This wasn't the regular crew of men and, unfortunately, none of them realized that the seat cushions doubled as life jackets. They also didn't know that the south shore of the lake was the wrong direction to swim. To them it looked closer, but the north, town-side had a shallow bench that reached to a few feet from the plane, which was sinking quickly into seventy-one feet of water. If it had come down just 100 feet closer, it would have landed in five feet of water.

Gordon and George sped toward the men as the RCMP boat shoved off from shore. One of the two policemen in the boat was Harold Macdonald, who later married Gordon's sister, Doris. Incidentally, these were the only two boats that had not been pulled up for the winter, as the weather had been exceptionally harsh that year.

This day it was bright and shiny, but very cold. One of the fellows ahead was coming up for the third time as they approached, but when they reached him, he was on his way down again. They could see him six to eight feet under the water. Gordon bailed out over the side to try to reach him. George grabbed his ankle and held fast as Gordon was lucky to just reach the man's upstretched wrist. Later the man said it was the best handshake he had ever felt. George pulled Gordon up over the side and he, in turn, hauled the man up after him. He slumped down in the boat, unconscious. There was no time to check whether he was alive, because ahead they could see another man who had been treading water start to sink. They reached him just in time. Then they headed for another thrashing swimmer. Together, the two boats rescued six men of the seventeen. One of them was Captain Boray, the copilot. McWilliams, the Flight Captain, had already gone to the bottom with the rest of the men.

I had been standing with other townsfolk on the walk bridge that spanned the lake a short distance from the disaster. The screams from those poor men upset me terribly. Apparently, the octane in the gas floating on the water from the plane burned their skin and was harder for them to bear than the cold water. Mrs. Grant, the minister's wife, bustled me into her house until it was over, as my baby was due in six weeks.

The house we were renting was a short distance from the bridge. Gordon thought it best to take the survivors there since Carcross had no hospital, nor even a first-aid station. Strangely enough, one of the rescued men was very thirsty, and kept asking for water to drink. One would think he would not want to see water again for the rest of his life! The men were deeply upset at the loss of their buddies, but physically, they were okay.

People in the railway station had also seen the accident and immediately sent a telegram to Whitehorse. The U.S. Air Force sent a doctor and a sergeant to Carcross in a Norseman aircraft to assist the survivors. Two ambulances also left Whitehorse but, in the rush, one rolled over a bank and only one arrived. The doctor checked the surviving men and said they were fine. He returned to hospital in the ambulance with them in case of after-shock.

The sergeant stayed overnight in Carcross, to go back with the pilot of the Norseman. It was getting too late in the day to fly to Whitehorse. The pilot also wanted to talk to Gordon about the particulars of the accident.

I remember how our sheets smelled of gasoline as I changed them that night. Trying to sleep after a day like that was almost impossible.

Gordon got up a couple of times to pace around, so finally I got up, too, to make a cup of hot chocolate for him. I kept thinking about all those bodies still on the bottom of the lake and wondered if their wives and families had received the news yet.

The next morning, as Gordon was leaving the house, we heard a plane take off from the airfield, a mile and a half across the lagoon.

"That will be the pilot of the Norseman flying back to Whitehorse with the sergeant," Gordon said to me. "It sure sounds odd, though…"

All of a sudden the motor stopped and there was a loud BOOM! We could see the burst of fire from where we stood. It had crashed!

Hugh Grant, an Anglican minister as well as superintendent of the Indian Residential School, lived next door with his family. Gordon gave him a call.

"We'd better get over to the airfield—looks like there's been another calamity."

They jumped into the pickup and took off, sending up a cloud of dust in their wake. At the airfield, the story unfolded.

The pilot took off but the plane went out of control and veered off the runway toward Northern Airway's hangar. It clipped two feet of wing off a parked Travel Air. They did gain the air, however, and would have stayed airborne except for an A-frame. This was really a high pole, slung with cables for lifting planes and motors around. The plane struck the heavy cables and hung up right there—exploding into a ball of flame. When Gordon and Pa Grant got there, the charred remains of the plane was still hanging on the wires. The fellows were still strapped in their seats, their skulls cracked open at the seams, and they were burned beyond recognition.

That tragic weekend saw the end of thirteen lives, two planes, and an ambulance.

Later, divers from Anchorage, Alaska, brought up the eleven bodies.

"In that icy cold water," Gordon said, "they hadn't a mark on them. They looked like they were only sleeping. Even their color was pink and healthy looking."

Using his own boat, which had an air compressor to supply oxygen to the divers, Gordon helped with the job as long as he could; but it wasn't easy. He was only too glad to hand the job over to the soldier who came to spell him off.

32

ordon & Joyce Yardley in 1942.   Joyce Yardley 1992.   *Photo: J. Neil Newton*

ain station at Taku Arm, Tagish Lake, in the Gold Rush days.

Photo: Courtesy of Yukon Archives

View of Lake Bennett from our house in Carcross.

Our house in Carcross in 1958.

rk's cabin on Discovery, Atlin, B.C. in 1979.

eft to right: Joe Jacquot, Gordon and Dave Small; sitting: Dorothy Vill, Bob Vill, and Joyce
front of cabin in 1968.

Stu Enderton & Gordon (on right) fishing at Ten-Mile Ranch in the late '40s.

t Ten-Mile Ranch on Lake Tagish. Emily Simmons & Joyce with freshly caught trout.

Wishful thinking! Ted with trout at Ten-Mile Ranch.

Dezadeash meadow in 1968.

Dezadeash Lodge in summer on the Haines Highway, Yukon, 1960–1968. It was a fully modern resort with excellent fishing.

Photo: J. H. Bell

Dezadeash Lodge in winter, 1960–1968.

Mr. & Mrs. Partridge at Ben-My-Chree.

White Pass paddle wheelers in Carcross. Gordon worked for five years on the *Tutshi* as a deckhand.
Photo: Courtesy of Yukon Archives

Beached on Lake Bennett in 1943.

↑ Rest stop. Ptarmigan tracks in the snow, 1968.

← Joyce & Gordon on the trapline in 1971.

↓ Dave Small suntanning, 1968.

Jimmy Kane & Chuck Keene, producer, on the set of *Challenge to be Free.*

Mike Mazurki & Joyce during the filming of *Challenge to be Free.*

Gordon (left) & Alex Van Bibber during the filming of *Challenge to be Free.*

Gold mining at Atlin between 1978–83.

→ Trommel and backhoe at Mount Freegold, Carmacks.

↓ Hazards of the job. All equipment to the rescue.

The first sluice box in operation at Atlin.

← Our second bigger and better sluice box.

↓ Old Engineer Mine in the early days on Tagish Lake.
Photo: Courtesy of Yukon Archives

The first stage of mining gold. Kurt Waddington pouring concentrate into the jig to separate the gold.

Heating the gold to dry it.

Blowing fine sand out of the gold.

Pouring gold into the crucible.

Mixing flux with gold in the crucible.

eady to fire the crucible.

► Removing from kiln about twenty minutes later. Molten gold in crucible.

After gold has cooled, the slag or impurities are removed from the brick.

Gold from the Atlin mine. Finished product. A miner's brick before cleaning.

Jimmy Kane, a Dalton Post Indian, leaving Klukshu with his pack train in 1948.

Photo: Courtesy of National Museums of Canada.

They decided to bring the Fortress up also; it looked as though it would be no problem to get a hook on it to bring it to the surface. The only catch was—the barge that the White Pass used for freight was on the wrong side of the bridge.

In Carcross, the railway goes through the upper end of town and over a bridge which spans a short river that joins Tagish and Bennett lakes. Another walk bridge starts halfway down the row of buildings that line the beach frontage. It is a rickety wooden structure, with a railing on both sides, spanning the same river. Tourists and town people stand there and fish in the summertime for freshwater herring, which pass under the bridge by the thousands.

Tagish Lake lays in an arc, to the east of Carcross, then in a southerly direction for eighty miles. Lake Bennett stretches southwest for twenty-four miles, ending forty miles from Skagway, Alaska. This was the route traveled by the prospectors and miners on their way to Dawson City and the Klondike in 1898.

The main obstacle to salvaging the Fortress seemed to be getting the barge under the walk bridge. The railway bridge did not pose a problem. Nobody had a solution, so they came to Gordon to ask his advice, as he was familiar with the territory. Always keen for a challenge like this, Gordon agreed to oversee the operation.

A friend of his also had a boat, the same size as ours. They put both in the water, hoping that two boats could push the barge under the railway bridge and along to the other one. This plan worked fine. So far so good. Now for the clever part: they filled the barge with water until it was submerged enough to go under the walk bridge, then they pumped the water back out and pushed it to shore.

The U.S. Army loaned them a "Diamond T" wrecker, which they drove onto the barge. With the two boats, they pushed barge, wrecker and all, to the spot where the Fortress lay in seventy feet of water. The divers got a hook on it, and the wrecker sucked the plane up to the surface with the cable. They pushed the whole works toward shore and dropped the plane on the shallow bench of sand in about five to six feet of water. Next, they drove the wrecker off the barge onto the land and tried to winch the plane out. The weight was too much, however, so they had to get still another wrecker to give them enough power to drag the plane up onto the beach with two sets of cables. They took the wings off, dismantled what was necessary in order to load it onto trucks, and hauled everything into Whitehorse.

The Air Force salvaged the motors, but never did get the plane rebuilt. The Flying Fortress lay on the edge of the Whitehorse Airfield for six or eight years. One day, as we were driving by, we noticed that it was in flames. They had decided to burn it.

A day or two after the crash, by some strange stroke of fate, there arrived in the mail some wartime literature filled with the latest news and information. One of the articles was entitled something like, "How to Beach a Flying Fortress if Necessary," and told about feathering the props at the correct time, when to shut off the motors, et cetera. The timing of this article was ironic.

Gordon received an official letter of thanks from the United States Air Force for his part in saving the lives of the men who, otherwise, would not have made it.

Our Trip "Outside"

In those years, most of the people lived on the north side of the lake, in a long row of very old log houses stretching from the railroad bridge to the sand dunes at the west end of town. The majority of these cabins were owned by Matthew Watson, the local store owner, who had been renting them out for years.

Not quite fitting into the mold, we had arrived on the scene as young upstarts, building our own house at the end of the row. Actually, we were all squatters on that street as the property was classed as waterfront and we couldn't buy it.

Opinion was divided on whether or not to pressure the government into allowing us to purchase legal rights to the land. It was many years later that the land was actually released. Lots could be purchased across the gravel road that ran alongside the houses, however, and we bought one of these, right across from our house, thinking maybe it would be a good investment at some future date.

50

Meanwhile, I waited impatiently for our baby to arrive. When the time came, though, it still caught me unprepared. Around seven in the evening, on December 5, the first little gnawing pains began. For a while, I didn't know what they were. A couple of hours later, they were a lot stronger and were coming with regularity.

Thoughts went racing through my mind. 'The doctor said not for two more weeks.' 'Why doesn't Gordon get back here?' 'I'd better pack some clothes.'

Really scared now, I stuffed some things into a suitcase and put on my heavy coat and mukluks. I was just starting out the door to find someone—anyone—who could tell me what to do, when Gordon arrived.

He took one look at my face and said, "Are you okay? What happened?"

"The baby's coming. We have to get to the hospital!"

"Get in the pickup then and let's go," he told me, not even stopping to pick up his razor or toothbrush.

We had fifty miles to drive and there was no time to lose. Even though he drove as fast as safety allowed, it was the longest trip I'd ever made to Whitehorse over that winter road. I remember the clanking sound of the snow chains that Gordon was using on the tires.

'Please, God, don't let us get a flat tire!' I prayed.

As it turned out, we need not have hurried so much. I was still in labor eighteen hours later. Exhausted, I would immediately drop into a deep sleep between the contractions, which kept jerking me awake.

'Nobody told me,' I kept thinking. 'Why didn't someone tell me it would be like this?' I felt that life had betrayed me. The nurse's voice seemed to come from a great distance.

"I think we should give her something now," one of them said. "It doesn't look like the doctor's going to get here."

When I woke up, it felt as if I had been away somewhere for a long time. The room was not familiar; everything was blurry. Force of habit made me reach for my glasses on the table beside the bed. The movement hurt—a lot. Memory came flooding back. 'The baby—where's my baby?'

51

Just as panic began to grab me by the throat, the nurse entered the room, carrying a small bundle wrapped in a pink blanket. She put her into my arms...and the world stood still. I gazed at the tiny features of this perfect little child, and breathed in her wonderful aroma. She was squirming around seeking hungrily. The nurse put her to my breast. I felt that my whole life had been leading up to this one indescribable experience of holding my first child. She was infinitely worth all the racking pain and screams that had preceded her. I reluctantly handed her back to the nurse, who came to take her back to the nursery. 'I couldn't go through it again, though,' I thought drowsily before dropping into a deep, happy sleep.

When I opened my eyes, Gordon was sitting alongside the bed in a chair he'd pulled up close. The last thoughts I had gone to sleep with were the first unplanned words to slip out as he leaned over to kiss my forehead.

"One baby is all we need, isn't it? Especially as she's so beautiful!"

Gordon must have detected a note of anxiety in my voice.

"Of course one is enough," he agreed emphatically.

We named her Norma Dale. She was born on December 6, 1943, and weighed eight pounds, four ounces. She was also born in the same room in the same hospital where I had come into the world eighteen years earlier. One of the nurses in attendance was the same person who had helped to deliver me. Mrs. Howatt was actually retired from her job as matron in the hospital but she was called back from time to time when the hospital needed extra help.

It was ten days before they finally let me go home—which was not unusual with childbirth back then—and the pain was all but forgotten.

I even found myself saying things like, "We won't buy a cheap high chair, we'll get one that we can use again later."

In January, 1944, when Norma was six weeks old, we took her to Vancouver to meet her grandparents. It was the first trip outside for me, as I couldn't remember much about the time I'd gone out with my parents at three and a half years old. Luckily, Norma was as good as gold.

Gordon likes to tell stories on me about that trip.

There were no neon signs in Whitehorse, and we referred to cities out of the Territory as "Outside" or the "Bright Lights." It was evening when we arrived in Skagway and we checked into a hotel. There was a sign above the door that said Pack Train Inn. Three 40-watt light bulbs were encased in a glass box-type fixture, and painted on the inside of the glass was a pack train of horses out on the trail.

"Boy!" I sighed, "it sure feels good to be out in the Bright Lights."

The next day we boarded ship, the S.S. *Princess Norah*. They took great pride in the service they offered and the meals were done in style. The waiter hovered nearby to make sure your every wish was granted. One of them noticed at breakfast that I hadn't touched my eggs or the milk I'd asked for.

"Is something wrong with the eggs, ma'am?" he inquired.

"Well," I answered, "they don't have much flavor."

No one raised chickens in Whitehorse, and by the time the freight arrived in town, the eggs were a bit flavorful.

"And the milk, madam?" he asked.

"It tastes a bit odd, too," I admitted.

Gordon suggested that I'd probably enjoy some canned milk diluted with water, if they had any; and sure enough, it was served a minute or two later on a silver tray.

On the deck after sundown that evening, the air felt balmy after the forty below we'd left behind. It was a lovely night and we stood there enjoying it, watching the lights flicker off and on.

"Are we near shore?" I asked.

"No," Gordon said. "Those are just buoys and the lights are a guide to small boats."

"Gosh," I marveled. "It must really keep that fellow busy, turning them off and on."

I never heard the last of that one.

I wasn't sure what to expect when we reached Vancouver. There was no television in those days with travel documentaries to prepare one in advance and pictures in books don't convey dimensions that well. I was amazed at the magnitude of the city and the lights on Granville Street.

"What do you think of the big city?" Gordon asked.

"Well," I answered, "these trails are sure wide!"

We arrived at the home of Gordon's parents in Langley, where we stayed for a week or so while they got to meet their new granddaughter, and their daughter-in-law.

Gordon's mom was enthralled with the baby. She'd get up in the middle of the night to make sure Norma was covered, just as she'd always done with her own kids; then she'd come into our room and cover Gordon and me, too, whether we needed it or not.

She was such a considerate person and she loved to fuss over us. I appreciated her good intentions, although I used to wish she'd confine the covering part to the baby; it was a bit disconcerting at times, never knowing when she'd come tiptoeing into our room to make sure we were covered.

Here is another story that Gordon likes to tell on me. True, I'm afraid.

On our first morning at Gordon's parents, as daylight was breaking, I was awakened by a strange sound outside. It sounded like someone groaning in pain. Suddenly alert, I lay there listening intently, straining my ears. Sure enough, it came again.

"Gordon," I called. "Wake up—there's been an accident. Someone's groaning outside there by the road!"

"You're imagining things," he muttered sleepily, and rolled over, pulling the covers over his head.

"No, no!" I insisted, shaking him some more. "You just listen...there it is again. Someone's been hurt!"

Reluctantly, he sat up in bed. The groans began again, a little louder.

"Is that what you heard?" he asked.

"Yes, do something quick!"

"Go back to sleep," he replied. "It's only the chickens."

"*Chickens?* I thought they said, 'Cock-a-doodle-do.' "

"Whatever gave you that idea?"

"Well," I answered, "that's what it says in the book."

I'd never seen or heard chickens before. Gordon's dad, Pop, being a thrifty soul, kept a dozen in the backyard so they'd have fresh eggs for the two of them. I guess the chickens were just waking up and starting to stir, but it sounded for all the world like someone in pain.

Gordon's dad was in the hardware business in Langley. They moved there from Radville, Saskatchewan, when Gordon was seventeen. Listening to him talking with his parents, I learned something of his early life on the prairies.

3

Kid from the Prairies

Flashback

Gordon was born in 1917 at Estevan, Saskatchewan. Estevan is on the Soo Line, which runs between Moose Jaw in Canada and Minneapolis in the United States. It is almost on the border.

When he was school age, the family moved to Radville, eighty miles away. During the drought and Great Depression in the thirties, Gordon's dad was in the implement business.

"Were you able to get any work out of Gordon in those days, Pop?" I asked him.

"Well, he was out thrashing in 1929 when he was twelve for a dollar a day," Pop said. "He worked on a big steam outfit with a couple of his friends; one of them was thirteen and I guess the other kid was a year older, wasn't he, boy? During the depression, a lot of kids had to leave school and go to work. We wouldn't let Gordon quit, but sometimes he'd take a couple of weeks off from school when a job came up."

"We didn't make much money but we had a lot of fun, just the same," Gordon said. "Some of those larger outfits had their own bunk cars and cookhouses. The food on those thrashing crews was something to write home about. We had to load bundles that were twenty to thirty pounds each. Our wrists would get so sore when we first started the job that in the mornings we'd have to soak our hands in warm water to get our fingers mobile. We wore leather bands on our wrists the first few days, but once we got used to the work it was okay and we didn't need them anymore."

"I put him to work in his spare time, assembling machinery," Pop said. "Mostly tractors and combines. Remember the old French farmer, the one who owned the thirteen quarters of land?

56

He noticed you and me assembling combines one day. He came over and said, 'Tom, I want that boy of yours to run my combine for me.' "

"Wasn't he awfully young for a job like that?" I asked Pop.

"Not me!" said Gordon.

"Oh, quit your bragging, I'm asking your dad," I retorted.

"Well, I told the farmer he was much too young for the job—he was only fourteen years old. But he said, 'I've watched him putting them together. He can handle it; if he can put 'em together he can run 'em!' "

Gordon took the job. He now got double the pay, two dollars a day.

"So, you were really coming up in the world," I said to Gordon. "What did you do for fun?"

"Oh, on Sundays my pals and I made racing cars out of Model A's and T's. Also, there were schoolhouses all over the country where they used to throw some pretty lively dances on Saturday nights. There were no jobs available, so people got together a lot more in those days than they do now. They had jam sessions and pot-luck dinners and lots of dances."

Many farmers had no money for gas to attend these functions, but they did have ingenuity. Some took the motors out of their cars and attached a "pole hitch" to them so they could hook up a team of horses and use them like buggies. These, in fact, were what they used to call Bennett Buggies in those days.

"Did you have one of those?" I asked Gordon.

"No," he replied. "I had a bike. Model A's had a value of fifty dollars. A bunch of them ended up back at the dealers. So my friends and I would wheel and deal in cars, and pick up some money that way. And we trapped muskrats, which brought one or two dollars a pelt. On Saturdays, we'd catch a ride with a farmer on his way home, and ride about three miles out of town with him. Then we'd jump out and work the ditches alongside the road collecting beer bottles. We used to find lots of them behind dance halls and in the dump."

Eventually, Gordon had enough money to buy a new deluxe bicycle for forty-five dollars. A businessman at fourteen years old!

"Was the story about the goat that Gordon and his friend Art Hoff bought true, Pop?" I wanted to know. "Or was he just putting me on?"

Pop loved to tell stories. His version varied a bit from Gordon's, but the gist of it was the same.

The boys had bought a billy goat which became a real pet and followed them wherever they went. Whenever there was a hockey game at the skating rink, the two boys would go. Because money was so scarce, they would find a spot on the snowpiles along the fence where they were mostly hidden from view and could watch the games. The goat always went along too, sitting between them. In time, it became fascinated by the black puck on the ice— shooting back and forth in all directions. He would actually swivel his head back and forth like a metronome—never taking his eyes off the puck.

At one of these games, a policeman happened to notice the boys and started toward them with the intention of making them either leave or buy a ticket. The boys spotted him coming and beat it, expecting the goat to follow as usual. Instead, it was so intent on watching that puck that it didn't notice them going. The policeman gave the animal a nudge with his foot. This startled the goat and it began moving away. The officer turned and started back; but unknown to him, the goat suddenly changed its mind. It turned around and made a run for the man, putting down its head and butting him hard in the rear. The policeman was knocked head over heels. The boys, who watched from a distance, rolled over and over on the snow in evil mirth.

"So, you wouldn't take my word for it, eh?" Gordon chided.

"Just checking up on you," I answered.

Gordon's mom now joined in, telling us a story about an old farmer who had approached Pop in Radville one day wanting to buy a tractor.

"I don't have no trade in, but I got a good milk cow here," he said.

"I haven't a place to keep a cow," Pop told him. "I'm sorry."

The old man looked disappointed, but he was proud.

"Well then, I'm not giving you the business. This here's a good cow and she's all I have handy right now." He turned to go.

"Wait a minute."

Pop reflected that his tractors weren't selling anyway and the old fellow sure could use one right now.

"Okay," he said. "Tie her up out there and we'll figure something out."

When he came home that night for dinner, Tom told the family what had transpired.

"Now what do we do with the thing?" he wondered ruefully.

Gordon, always looking for an opportunity to make some money, began thinking of all the things he could do with a milk cow. He had managed to save twenty-two dollars from thrashing, at one dollar a day.

"I'll buy her from you, Pop," he offered. "But I only have twenty-two dollars right now."

"It's a deal," his dad told him. "But you'll have to find some place to keep her when winter comes."

So, Gordon now owned a twenty-two dollar milk cow. It was with great excitement that he discovered the cow was in calf, and in a short time he was the proud owner of a little heifer, as well. He kept it out on the range until fall.

Soon, he heard of a wheat farmer who had moved into town, where it was handier for his children to go to school in the winter months. He was renting a house which included an old barn. He heard about the fresh cow that Gordon had, and suggested that he could keep her in the barn and look after her.

At the same time, a friend of this farmer, who had also moved his family to town, offered to supply the hay and feed and suggested dividing the milk three ways. Gordon got a gallon a day for his share, which his Pop offered to buy for twenty-five cents; so he was in business again.

When spring came, he had to decide on a new plan for the cow and calf, as the farmers were moving back to the country.

There was a Mountie in town who had just retired and gone into the small farming and dairy business. He offered to look after the cow, as he was shipping cream. This agreement carried on for several years, and during this time the first calf had produced one of her own, plus the original cow had produced two more calves, making a total of five head.

59

About that time, Pop decided to move his family to the west coast where cattle, like farm equipment, was almost valueless. There was nothing left to do but sell the herd. The cream shipper offered Gordon thirty-five dollars for the five head of cattle. So ended his first successful ranching endeavor.

In 1934, the family moved to the coast and opened a hardware store in Langley, B.C.

Gordon had left school by this time. He got a part-time job with the mill in Fort Langley and helped his dad in the store the rest of the time.

"Is that what you worked at right until you came to the Yukon?" I asked him.

"No, in June of '35 I had a chance to go and drive a truck for an outfit back in Saskatchewan. The only way I could go was to ride the rails, not having any extra cash. When I hitched a ride into Vancouver, I sure wasn't expecting the crowd that was there at the train waiting to board the boxcars. They turned out to be the "on-to-Ottawa" trekkers that were staging a demonstration to protest the lack of jobs in Canada. There were 1,400 of them. I rode with them as far as Calgary. They were going to stay there for a day, but I had to keep going, or I wouldn't have got to the job on time."

"What was it like on the roof of the boxcars?"

"It was okay until we got to Revelstoke. It got pretty frosty up there in the mountains at night. Some of us walked ahead until we reached the 'tender,' and that was almost too warm. If I was lying on my back, my belly would freeze; and if I rolled over, it was too hot and it felt like the goose bumps on my back were standing up an inch high."

"Didn't the smoke burn your eyes in the tunnels?" I asked.

"Well, I had to pull my wool sweater up over my face, then my leather jacket over my head till we were out again. I sure didn't realize this trek was going to turn into the bloody Regina Riot, when these guys arrived. That was one I'm happy to have missed!"

And that was one story I had missed hearing about in the Yukon, but at the age of nine it was hardly likely that I would have realized the tragedy of that notorious historical event.

The rest of Gordon's story I knew by heart. In 1937, he had a job offer which was too good to resist—a chance to work on a sternwheeler, the S.S. *Tutshi,* which was based in Carcross, as a deckhand. He lost no time packing his bags and heading north. He worked on the paddle wheeler for five summer seasons before going to work with Pan American World Airways.

Keep 'em Flying

While Gordon had been working on the *Tutshi,* some of the White Pass officials had their cars rigged with special wheels made for running on the railroad tracks. The main base for the company was in Whitehorse, of course, but they would come over to Carcross to check on their *Tutshi* operation.

Even though they had an engineer and second engineer who were qualified for steamwork on the boat, these men didn't have the right kind of training to do any maintenance work on these track cars.

So Gordon would offer to take on the job for something to do if there was time between sailings.

The job offer with Pan American came as a surprise. He figured that someone had put in a good word for him. It was double his current pay.

As he was not a qualified mechanic—though he had been puttering around with old cars and equipment since he was a child—he phoned from the train station to tell the manager of Pan American that he had no experience with aircraft.

Joe Morrison, the manager, phoned back to say, "Don't worry about it. We'll train you our way when you get here. But you'll have to be on the job in a week to ten days at the latest."

This was the year I had met Gordon.

Pan American was a U.S. airline flying up through the Yukon. They had established a route from Seattle, up the coast to Juneau, Alaska, then on to Whitehorse, Yukon, and Fairbanks, Alaska. Whitehorse was the main base because it was a halfway point. The planes could fly from Seattle to Whitehorse in one day, overnight there, then go on to Fairbanks next day, and sometimes back again to Whitehorse.

61

The company had four planes. They started out with two Lougheed Electras, which were ten-passenger planes. Then they bought two Lodestars, which held fourteen passengers each.

When the trouble began with the Japanese, the U.S. Air Force and U.S. Navy planes started flying to Alaska. Pan American had taken on the responsibility of servicing them all, including the fighters going through to Russia. The Navy pilots would take these as far as Fairbanks, where they'd hand them over to the Russian pilots, who would take them off to Umsk. Flight after flight came in to the airfield, so they were very busy.

Part of Gordon's job was to keep the planes operational and in the cold weather, heating them up. At first, they had torch blowers or pots that burned white gas. These were manufactured in Seattle and shipped up. If the planes had to leave by 8:00 A.M., he and his fellow mechanics would have to be at the airfield by 4:00 A.M. to put the torch blowers on.

Having no hangars then, the only way they could handle the planes was to run them up on ramps, which were wired with electricity to keep the oil warm. Then they made big heaters, which they placed under the motors. They wrapped canvas around them like a tent—sometimes they would have to place three torch blowers together to generate enough heat to be effective in such extreme temperatures as forty degrees below zero.

Every once in a while, one of these blowers would go out and cool off. This caused it to throw a jet of raw gas onto the motors. The other blowers would reignite it, which created a fire. To keep the plane from burning up, the men had to camp right on it.

There were only two men who were in charge of that operation; Gordon was one. In between all this, Gordon also helped to service the U.S. fighter planes. Later, Pan Am provided some portable oil-type furnaces for heating the airline motors. Now the men could heat the planes and heads, check the oil temperature, and fill the fuel tanks.

Sometimes Gordon would even get to taxi the aircraft to the administration building so when the Pan Am pilots arrived at the airport in the morning with their passengers, the planes were ready for takeoff.

Often, on the return route to Seattle, there was limited visibility around Juneau and the planes would sometimes have to be turned back to Whitehorse to wait it out.

They would leave the base on the first leg to Juneau with a full tank of fuel. If Juneau was fogged in, the pilots had three alternatives: Dease Lake and Telegraph Creek, B.C., or Whitehorse. With no radar, takeoff and landing was by sight only. They could see, when only a few minutes in the air, whether Juneau was clear or not. But they had not yet used enough of their fuel that they could land safely—so they'd dump most of it before trying. Then the big birds would have to be fueled up again, sometimes within an hour, for another try.

Gordon had received his basic training for the Canadian Army—compulsory in the 1940s as part of the national preparedness—in Vernon, before taking the job with Pan American. Now his job was considered essential to the war effort so he never went off to fight. He worked for the airways for two years; it was during this time that we were married.

Our reminiscing with Gordon's parents in Langley at an end, we prepared for our trip home via the *Princess Norah* to Skagway, then by train to Carcross.

4

Life in Carcross

After our trip to Vancouver with the baby, it was back to work again. The pole contract had been a good one, but now we had to try other sources of income. In the 1940s, there was no such thing as unemployment insurance.

There was a shortage of firewood in town. The original supplier was getting on in years and found the job too strenuous. Gordon began cutting the trees and hauling them into town with his truck. Some people would buzz up their own cordwood and others would get Gordon to do it with his power saw. He also started hauling barrels of stove oil from Whitehorse for several families who were heating their houses with oil heaters. At the same time, he brought liquor for the local Caribou Hotel and the Carcross Inn.

The gravel road to Whitehorse was decent by this time. If you were lucky, you could make it in a day. On the old trail, it sometimes took three days to go the fifty miles; and you needed a vehicle with high wheels and lots of clearance.

George Dale

One of our neighbors was an old fellow by the name of George Dale. Gordon had known him for some time and had persuaded the old gent to move into a cabin close to us so we could keep an eye on him. The rheumatism in his legs was getting worse.

Previously, George had lived in a little cabin a mile or two from town on the lakeshore, where he had raised mink for many years. He had been a prospector when he was young and had staked the famous old Comstock Mine in Virginia City, Nevada, with two partners when he was sixteen years old. They made

$240,000 between them, a very large sum of money. Later, he and a partner got $120,000 for some iron ore claims in Montana.

Gordon asked him, "How long did that money last you, George?"

"Well," he said, "I thought it would last forever, but— about three years I guess. After that I came to Carcross and sold some old Venus Mine claims to Colonel Conrad. Got $42,000 each on that deal."

"What happened to all that money?" Gordon inquired, as it was obvious that the man was living on rations.

"Oh, I thought it was time to visit the city again, so I bought me a brand new suit and set out for Las Vegas. I'll tell you, boy, by spring I was sure getting lonesome for the Yukon. Trouble was, I still had some of that 'stuff' left (meaning money).

"I didn't want to cart that back with me, so I hatched up a scheme to get rid of it and have a pile of fun at the same time. Went to the bank and took out $1,000 in dimes; took it over to a busy intersection in the city and threw it out into the street. What a panic! People on their knees grabbing the money up—brakes squealing—and drivers getting out of their cars to join the throng. Talk about fun; had the traffic tied up for half a day!"

Eventually, he had spent it all. He didn't seem to miss it, though. Now he was content to stay indoors with his books and wood heater.

Gordon went to see him often, as he was good company, extremely well read, and a born philosopher. An old photograph on his table showed George at a younger age in a tailored suit, looking like a young executive.

Most old-timers seemed to be either excessively clean or the reverse. George had too much reading to do to worry about housework. The old kerosene lamp beside his bed had a chimney that was black with soot. It made you wonder how he could read by it for hours on end without ruining his eyesight. He never used eyeglasses. He did use his broom, however. He kept a clean path swept through the cabin; it went from the bed, around the small lamp stand, angled over to the kitchen table, and went around the stove and wood box to the door. On either side of this path, built up about three feet on each wall, was a pile of wood chips, tin cans, newspapers, and debris. The books and papers formed a pile that was level with the top of his mattress and gradually sloped down to the floor.

George used to wear Stanfield underwear, with the long arms and legs, that he didn't bother changing. The day came when Gordon decided he would have to mention it to the old man. "Think it's time you took them off, George, and soaked them in some soapy water."

"Yes," George said. "I've been thinking about it but I think it's too late now, they'd never come clean."

"Oh, sure they would, just go over to Matthew Watson's and get a can of lye. Put a little in the wash water and boil them on the stove in a tub. That'll fix them."

"Well, I might try that," George said.

When Gordon went over a few days later, he noticed that the old man had on a new suit of Stanfields.

"How did your washing turn out, George?" he asked him.

"Well, by golly, I took your advice. I figured if a little would do it—a whole can should work better yet. Works real good, only have to do it once. I boiled them a while and the only thing left in the tub was the buttons!"

One day, as Gordon and I walked to the store, we saw George sitting on the edge of the sidewalk talking to a tourist who had apparently asked him what he used to do for a living.

"Oh, I did a little prospecting," George was saying.

"Did you have any success?"

"Well I made $42,000 on the last property sale."

"Did that satisfy you?" the tourist wanted to know. "Or did you have a craving to make more?"

George threw up his hands.

"God, no! That was enough. Just ten dollars more would've killed me!" (The price of a bottle of rum then.)

In all the years that George had lived in the Yukon, he had never been to Dawson City. He knew there was an old folks' home there, though, and he was determined that he was never going to end up there. But as his legs got worse, he couldn't get around any more. He had to move to Whitehorse, where they looked after him in the hospital. It was Whitehorse's only facility for the elderly. George's mind was still as clear as crystal and he'd lay there and read (when he wasn't teasing the nurses). Gordon used to go to see him when he went to Whitehorse. George was around ninety-five then. One day, Gordon mentioned to a friend that he thought he'd go in tomorrow.

"George Dale?" the man asked. "He passed away about a month ago."

"Well, it's too late for that, then," said Gordon.

He felt a sense of loss and disappointment that he wouldn't see George one more time. It was about two weeks after that when a young brakeman on the railroad had an accident and ended up in the Whitehorse hospital. Gordon was in town and decided to drop in to see him.

The fellow was in the men's ward with six or eight other patients and while Gordon was standing there talking, his eyes wandered around the room. Lo and behold, there was George Dale, as large as life, in one of the beds—sitting up reading.

Gordon went over and said, "By gosh, George, I haven't been in to see you for a long time—but someone told me you'd passed away."

Old George looked around furtively, then put a finger over his lips.

"Sh!" he said in a loud whisper. "I think they've lost my number!"

He grinned mischievously. George lived to be six months short of a hundred.

Maude and Emerson Edwards

Among our friends in Carcross were Maude and Emerson Edwards. They had met in Dawson City during the Gold Rush, in 1912. She was fifteen and he was thirty-five years old. It was love at first sight. She became a very young bride a few months later. They stayed in the Klondike area for almost thirty years, raising their daughter as they mined on Hunker Creek.

One day they took a trip to Carcross and were so taken with the beauty of the lakes and mountains that they decided to make it their home. We had met them in 1943, just before Norma was born, while we were still living in Johnny John's house.

It was obvious that they were as much in love now as when they first married. They rented one of the cabins down the road from us until they could build. We were friends immediately. Although there was a considerable age difference between us all, we couldn't have been more compatible. Maude and Emerson had an old-fashioned hospitality that warmed your heart and they took us under their wing as if we were their own.

The four of us went muskrat hunting every spring and had many boat rides and camping trips together.

Aunt Maude, as we called her, was a tall, angular woman, with a Texan drawl. She wore her silver gray hair pulled back into a bun and usually tied with a scarf. When Norma arrived, she called her Baby Doll, and was forever sewing her little dresses— plus a lovely white parka, made from rabbit skins she had tanned herself.

Uncle Emerson was shorter, with a stocky build. He had a deep voice and a characteristic chuckle, which surfaced often, as he told us many tales of their pioneering days in the mining camps up north. Looking back, I realize that we were still pioneering at the time, and for some years to come.

In 1944, Maude and Emerson, their little dog Spotty, Gordon, myself, six-month-old Norma, and Moe Grant, the minister's teenaged son, went on a trip up Lake Bennett's West Arm in our boat. We wanted to look at the old site where the Partridges from Ben-My-Chree used to have their sawmill. It was a clear summery day with no wind. We had an enjoyable trip and did some fishing at West Arm.

On the way home, a sudden squall came up. In no time, the lake became so rough that we were in danger of being swamped if we didn't change direction, so we headed for the west shore. This was a long way off our destination. We knew there were big rocks close to that shore but we had no choice. The boat kept rising on a big wave—then the bow would SLAP down hard in the trough as the wave broke. Time after time, other waves crested, lifting us high—then DOWN we'd plunge again. When the next big one would approach from behind, we'd know that this one was going to wash right over the boat and drown us all. The only course available to us was to run against the breakers, toward the opposite shore, to keep the boat in a straight line—and hope for the best.

Moe was a rough and tough kid in those days, one who would rather die than show any signs of weakness; but I saw his lips moving and his eyes closed. I knew he was praying.

Uncle Emerson and Aunt Maude had been at opposite ends of the boat, but he came back to sit close and put his arm around her. I sat there clutching Norma, who was all bundled up in her blanket and sleeping peacefully. All I could think was, 'What if the boat capsizes and we lose her?' The spray was hitting us in the face with every slap of the boat, so no one noticed that I was crying. Gordon was so busy at the wheel that he didn't have time to worry about anything else.

At last we were close to the shore and could see the jagged rocks—hidden when the angry waves lashed over them, then exposed for a minute when the waves subsided.

By a streak of good fortune and good navigating on Gordon's part, we managed to avoid them. As soon as we reached waist-deep water, the men jumped in and guided the boat close to shore. The rest of us got out and hiked up the beach. Just then, a large breaker rolled in, lifted the boat, and deposited it high and dry on shore.

Moe got a fire started by rubbing two sticks together. We knew from experience that the storm would be over and the lake calm again by five or so in the morning; so we dried off by the fire. I filled Norma's bottle from the thermos and we settled down on the sandy beach for the night.

A couple of hours later, I woke up, changed the baby, and noticed that the wind had gone down a lot. Spotty, the little dog, was wide awake and running around, dragging something in his mouth. I gasped out loud when I saw what it was. He had the baby's one and only milk bottle, and was chewing on the nipple, which was already torn in half. The milk had all spilled out. I thought, 'If the wind comes up again, maybe we'll all starve to death.'

Luck was with us. When we woke at daybreak, the lake was like glass. What a welcome sight! In a couple of hours, we were home. Breakfast had never tasted so good.

Rafting Down the Lake

The Engineer Mine, at the south end of Tagish Lake, was shut down. It was abandoned except for the caretakers, Fred Ackles and his wife, who made it their home. The company was selling the townsite buildings, in August, 1944. Gordon left to put a bid in for a couple of them, which included a large warehouse. His bid was accepted. Uncle Emerson volunteered to help him dismantle them—he was in his seventies then.

So Emerson, Aunt Maude, Gordon, the baby, and I set off down Tagish Lake in our boat. We set up housekeeping in one of the vacant houses while the dismantling was taking place. Maude and I picked berries and baked pies. She taught me how to bake bread—properly. We also helped the men sort the lumber into piles and filled pails with the nails we pulled out of it. We salvaged 40,000 feet of good fir lumber from the bunkhouse, including the door and window cases. We formed these into bundles and tied them with rope that the men found on the site.

Gordon thought about getting the White Pass barge to ferry the lumber to Carcross, but their charge was going to be $400. Fred Ackles had several boats, including one that he never used. He offered to sell it to us for $400 and a deal was made right there. It was a double-ender, pointed at both ends, that was designed for an inboard motor. This one had a 490 Chevrolet motor in it.

We formed the lumber into a huge raft and made a temporary camp aboard it by pitching tents to sleep in and setting up a three-burner gas camp stove to cook on. Aunt Maude made bannock and hotcakes. I washed the dishes in the hand basin we'd brought along. Between meals, I suntanned on the lumber, snuggled up on my sleeping bag, and read books.

It took us seventy-two hours of towing at two miles per hour to get home. We never stopped and the boat never missed a beat.

I almost did, though. We had just rounded Squaw Point and, as Gordon was getting very sleepy, I volunteered to spell him off at the steering.

"See that peak, way over there behind Ten-Mile?" he asked, pointing.

"Just keep the nose of the boat right on that and you'll be fine. I'll take over before we get to Windy Arm."

By the time it got dark, everyone was sleeping and I ended up steering all the rest of the night. The dark shapes of the mountains showed up against the sky, which was lighter by contrast.

As we came closer to Ten-Mile, I had to abandon the peak that had been my guide or we'd have ended up getting too close to the shore. I decided not to wake Gordon, as he was very tired, and just keep a course straight down the middle of the lake.

I remember so clearly the Northern Lights that night. They provided me with fantastic entertainment during my solitary steering hours. Never had I seen such a display—rippling across the sky in huge waves of blue and crimson and gold—folding and unfolding in great curtains of color. Sometimes they came from opposite directions, receding and advancing with lightning speed, then merging directly overhead in a graceful arc—only to dance apart again. My spirit soared with them. I'd never felt wider awake than at that moment. When Gordon woke up, we were almost through Windy Arm.

It often got very rough crossing that arm; a strong wind or squall could have made our passage miserable, maybe loosened our load. The realization made us gulp. But the lake was like glass this time.

The whole trip turned out to be a successful adventure.

The demand for lumber was so great that we didn't even have to haul it to Whitehorse. The builders came and got it with trucks. It was all gone in three days.

We celebrated by taking another holiday to Vancouver.

The Alaska Highway

My mother and father moved to Vancouver in the summer of 1943. In the fall of 1944, Gordon and I went to visit them. By this time, my parents had decided that the city wasn't for them and they wanted to move back to Whitehorse. We decided to buy a car in Vancouver and drive home over the Alaska Highway, taking Mom and Dad with us. The road was still known as the Alcan Highway and was still being used to carry military supplies

71

to Alaska; the memory was still fresh that the Japanese had briefly taken over Attu, Agattu, amd Kiska islands at the tip of the Aleutian Islands in 1942—indeed, that was the reason for building the highway.

The road hadn't been officially opened to civilians because the war was still on and there were no accommodations along the route. I'm almost certain that Mom and I were the first civilian women to make the trip and Norma the first baby.

Not sure what the regulations were, we decided we'd drive as far as Dawson Creek, to Mile 0, then take a reading on the situation. We arrived after dark and stopped at a little cafe to eat and to make plans. We heard the check gate was located a couple of miles north of town. After traveling that distance, we didn't want to take the chance of being turned back at the gate. There would likely be reams of red tape to go through and we were anxious to be on our way.

We decided that Mom and I and Norma would wait in the cafe while the men checked through the gate—if they could. They would then make the excuse that they had forgotten something in town and come back to pick us up. The gate man, we hoped, would recognize the car (there was so little traffic) and wave us on through.

As soon as the men left, the cafe owner started to close up for the night. We went outside and sat on a bench to wait for the men's return—talking in hushed voices in the dark. Norma must have sensed the suspense in our tones. I still remember the expression on her face—half scared and half excited—and her big eyes as she tried to peer past a beam of light from the cafe into the dark shadows beyond as if to ask, "Where Daddy go?" Half an hour later, they returned.

"All right, let's go," said Gordon.

"What did you tell them?"

"Oh, just that we'd left a couple of old bags in town and would run back and pick them up."

"Very funny!" I retorted.

It turned out that the officer in charge had given the men permission to make the trip, as they presumably had jobs waiting for them in Carcross. Gordon had refrained from mentioning the female members of the family. Dad and Gordon rode in front and the three of us got in the back. When we got close to the gate, we hunched down and pulled a canvas over ourselves.

I felt the car stop and Gordon warned in a low voice, "Now, don't anyone move back there, the guy's coming over—"

Just then Norma began to let out loud howls of protest at being penned up like this.

In desperation, I clapped my hand over her mouth, whispering, "Just one minute more, honey, and you can get up."

Luckily, the gate man didn't hear her, although he came right up to the car to wish the men bon voyage. It was the start of yet another adventure.

We ate our meals under Bailey bridges to keep out of sight as best as we could. The tent was pitched after dark with flashlights. We ducked our heads whenever an army jeep or a big 6 x 6 truck came lumbering by. It probably wasn't necessary, as every vehicle that drove by on that gravel road threw up so much dust you couldn't see anything anyway.

This came in handy during one incident. We had stopped to answer the call of nature. On our way back to the car, an army truck came roaring around a corner, sending up a cloud of dust in its wake. I stood frozen to the spot. Mom, without a moment's hesitation, flung herself to the ground and stayed there until the vehicle was out of sight. What good she thought that would do, I haven't figured out yet. Guess it was an involuntary reaction. But the driver never even glanced in our direction. We certainly had a lot of laughs on that trip.

I don't think there has been a year since then that Gordon and I haven't made at least one trip over the Alaska highway.

5

Bloody Awful

Togo was a small Oriental man who had worked on the railroad in Carcross during the 1930s. Now he lived on the lake seven miles from town, where he cut cordwood for the Indian Residential School. He grew his own vegetables and had become a hermit.

Togo had an Indian wife in town who was a habitual drinker. She had chased him away so often that he had given up on her. She had a girl and two boys by him. He was very fond of the kids but the only time he came to town was at Christmas and he gave them the money that he had earned in the past year, making sure they had gifts and a big Christmas dinner—which he cooked himself.

In the winter of '45, Togo did not show up during the holidays. When February arrived with still no sign of him, we became concerned. There were two police officers in town, Sergeant Dave Bolger and Constable Harold Macdonald. Gordon went to see Bolger and suggested they look into the matter.

"I'll send Mac to check it out," said Bolger.

The next day, Mac set out on snowshoes for the three-sided cabin Togo had built on a rock wall 500 feet from the lake. He returned with the news that there was not a track to be seen. He had not been able to find the cabin in the deep snow. He came to talk it over with Gordon.

"Bolger wants to try it again in the morning," he said. "I can't get away before noon—that will make us pretty late getting back."

"I'll take him out, if you want," Gordon volunteered. "I know right where the cabin is."

After Mac left, I turned to Gordon, fuming.

"Why does it always have to be you who goes to the rescue? Can't they ask someone else once in a while? I thought we'd do something together tomorrow. You said you were taking the day off!"

"Well, I have the truck for it and I know where the cabin's located. What could I say?"

"They could have used your truck by themselves, couldn't they?"

But he was already on his way out the door to fuel up for the trip the next morning. I heard the story later, when Gordon returned.

He and Bolger had found the cabin without problem. They saw that the path to the water hole had blown over with snow. Leaving the truck on the lake, they hiked up to the cabin. There the snow had also piled up in big drifts—one almost covering the door. They were pretty certain what they'd find once they had shoveled their way in.

Sure enough, there on the floor lay poor little Togo. He was face up and frozen solid, with one arm flung out to the side and the other folded over his chest. On the wall hung the calendar where he'd been marking off the days—the last one sometime in December. By all signs, he must have been taken ill and was too weak to stand; it appeared he had made a last effort to get up and stoke the wood heater, and had collapsed.

Bolger was a tall, very straight and dignified Englishman who never lost his poise. He had come prepared for the worst, with a small sleigh and a white canvas bag, just in case.

"Well, let's get him wrapped up," he said. "If you gather up his things in the sleigh, I'll slide him along in the canvas."

Togo was frozen to the dirt floor, though, and wasn't that easy to move. Apparently, there had been a thaw. Gordon found a small pole to use as a lever. When he pried on the corpse, it popped up from the floor like a flat wafer.

"Bloody awful!" said Bolger, as he tried to slide him into the bag.

It was hard to do—the one frozen arm stuck straight out at right angles. Bolger tied a rope to the canvas bag and put it over his shoulder. He went on ahead, dragging Togo along behind him. Gordon followed with the sleigh loaded with Togo's belongings. Every few feet, Bolger's grisly load would shift and the frozen, outstretched arm would dig into the snow like a plough. The Mountie had to use all his strength to slide his cargo along.

Sergeant Bolger was dressed in his RCMP uniform under his parka, including the official police hat. Every twenty feet, he'd stop, carefully push up the brim of that hot hat, and wipe the sweat from his brow; then he'd straighten the hat, just so, and go on some more.

Now and then he would glance back and mutter, "Bloody awful!"

At last, they came to the truck and loaded Togo and his few worthless belongings into the back. Back in Carcross, Mac arrived to help. Gordon left the two policemen to cope with the necessary arrangements. A couple of days later, Mac came over and we heard the rest of the story.

He and Bolger were faced with the dilemma of having to thaw Togo to get him into the coffin. With the arm extended, there was no alternative. But they couldn't take him to his wife's cabin, as that would upset the children. Besides, she wouldn't be very happy with an arrangement like that. There was no morgue in town, and the police barracks consisted of one small building.

Then Mac remembered an abandoned cabin across the river. It had a big barrel wood heater in it. So they hauled Togo to the cabin, built a huge fire, and left him to thaw out overnight. The next morning, he was still as frozen as ever. The old cabin had long ago lost all its chinking. There were holes in the roof and the temperature outside was thirty degrees below zero. Mac stoked the stove once more and propped the corpse up against a wooden box closer to the heat—all to no avail. Hours later, it was still in the same condition.

Bolger came over to assess the situation.

"Bloody awful!" he exclaimed. "Enough of this. Mac, I want you to take a handsaw and cut off that arm. We have to get this man buried and that's all there is to it."

"Well, sir," replied Mac. "You may be the boss and normally I'd take any orders from you. But I'm NOT cutting off that arm, sir. Dismiss me if you like."

They decided to go to the army camp and see if any of the men there would do the job for ten dollars. No takers. The cook, however, a hardy individual, was in dire need of whisky. He offered to do the job for a bottle of rye. The only kind available at the time was a terrible tasting brand called Kings Plate.

"I've cut up a lot of meat in my day," he said. "What's one more carcass?"

As the Mounties left the camp that afternoon, Mac looked relieved; Bolger had a greenish cast to his face.

"Bloody awful!" he muttered.

But, at long last, they were able to give old Togo a decent burial.

"Well, Mac, this is one experience you three men are not going to forget for a while," I said.

"You can say that again!" he replied. "It could only happen in the Yukon, eh Gordon?"

Ten-Mile Ranch

There was an abandoned telegraph-line trail along the shore of Tagish Lake. Down this trail, fourteen miles from Carcross, was a place called Ten-Mile Ranch.

In the early days, all the mileage on the lake was gauged from an RCMP post on the Tagish River, above the town of Tagish. The river connects Tagish Lake with Marsh Lake. It was part of the old Gold Rush Trail which terminated in Dawson City. The ranch was exactly ten miles from the old post and so became known as Ten-Mile Ranch. The only access was by boat or foot in the summertime. This is where old Ernie Butterfield lived.

When Gordon was working on the *Tutshi,* before I knew him, he and a friend used to hike in to visit Ernie on their days off. The old man raised mink and ran a few head of cattle. There were trails from the cabin to three large meadows, which teemed with wildlife—migrating birds in the spring, bears during the summer, and moose in the fall. The meadows were used for hay, dating back to the gold rush days, when Atlin was a busy mining town. Besides Atlin, there were other communities in need of hay, including the town of Discovery, seven miles east of Atlin, where gold was discovered. During the boom years, Discovery housed as many as 10,000 people.

Paddle wheelers hauled all the freight that was needed in the summer, to the railway at Taku Landing; but in the winter months, teams of horses took over hauling between Carcross and Atlin—across the frozen lake. The winter portage was a ten-mile stretch of trail, which connected Tagish and Atlin lakes, at Moose Arm thirty miles east of Ten-Mile Ranch. The lakes were busy highways at the turn of the century, turning Ten-Mile into a hive of activity. It was used as a roadhouse to accommodate the travelers and it supplied hay to feed the teams.

By 1915, many of the mining properties were worked out and the Atlin area lapsed into decline. A few miners still found enough gold and silver to make a living, though—until eventually the tourist trade began to prosper. The freighting over the lake continued on a much smaller scale both summer and winter until the Atlin road was built in 1949.

The roadhouse and haying business at Ten-Mile were history long before our time, and the teams had been replaced with Cat tractors. These could travel faster and longer distances in the wintertime, so a roadhouse was no longer needed. Cat skinners continued to freight over the ice for many years and were still stopping by the ranch to see if Ernie needed anything.

I had never been to Ten-Mile, so one day Gordon took me there in our boat. I fell in love with the ranch at once and could see that Gordon felt the same way. He had heard that it was up for sale—as I found out later. He had sneakily planned this trip to tempt me and I had fallen right into the trap.

"Let's buy it," I said. "Just think what it would be like to have all this land to ourselves. It would be a perfect place to bring up kids."

"Well, we'll have to give this a lot of thought," he replied, but I thought I detected a note of satisfaction in his voice.

In the spring of 1946, we bought the ranch building, some haying equipment, four cows with calves, two horses—one sorrel, one black—plus a harness for $750 from Jock Milne, who had taken over from Ernie. Later we were able to purchase the land, including 400 acres of meadow, from two sisters who lived in England, for $1,000. This sounds like a good deal today, but back then it was a lot of money.

Lady Luck smiled on us. A family named Nelson, from Atlin, decided just then that they preferred Carcross because they could drive the fifty miles to Whitehorse easily. The timing was perfect—we rented our house in Carcross to them and moved out to the ranch.

For the first year, we had to come and go across the lake, by boat in the summer—we had an eighteen-foot wooden clinker-built boat with an inboard motor, and by jeep in the winter after the ice had thickened.

It was a mile from our house to the school meadow. The Indian Residential School in Carcross once leased this meadow for putting up hay for their horses and cow.

In the spring, when our brood cows were calving, either Gordon or I would ride over to this meadow every day to check on them. The original brood cows produced calves every year and supplied us with milk and cream, and, thus, cottage cheese.

One day Gordon came back and said, "I'm not sure whether that last cow has lost her calf or not. Her bag is pretty swollen and I can't find her calf anywhere. We'll have to bring her in and milk her tomorrow if it doesn't show up."

The cow he was referring to was a nervous animal; every spring she would hide her calf. The other three didn't seem to bother doing that unless something scared them.

The next morning, Gordon stayed with the kids while I rode Sister over to the meadow. Sure enough, one of the cows didn't have a calf with her; but on examining her bag, it didn't look extremely full or distended to me, as it should have if she'd recently lost a calf.

'Something funny going on here,' I thought.

I rode away from the cattle—keeping my eyes on that cow—toward the thick willow bushes that bordered the meadow. She never raised her head. I came back to her and rode off into the bushes in another direction—still no reaction. My third try brought results. As I neared the willow, I saw her stop grazing and lift her head to watch me, her whole body stiff and tense. In another minute, she took off on a fast run—in our direction. When she reached us she never even slowed down, but ran right past into the bushes with a warning bawl. I followed her for 150 feet. Sure

79

enough, there was the little calf, all curled up in the grass where her mother had left her. I waited long enough for the worried mother to nuzzle her offspring, then rode off slowly, hoping she'd realize we meant them no harm.

Another time, as I rode into view of the meadow to check on the cows, my horse shied and gave a loud snort, almost bouncing me out of the saddle. Just as quickly, he settled down again. Ahead about 300 feet, was a large bear. I could tell by the hump on the neck and the sandy colored hair on its upper back that it was a grizzly. He was digging out gophers on the edge of the meadow and didn't pay the slightest attention to me or the horse. Neither did the Canada geese that were feeding on the meadow or the cows that grazed not more than 1,000 feet away. They seemed to be sharing the meadow in harmony. After taking a cattle count, I rode on home and told Gordon.

"Well, if they're not worried, I guess we shouldn't be," was his answer.

I noticed that he rode in that direction later in the day, although he wouldn't admit he'd been out to check on the cows.

The two smaller meadows on our property were connected by short trails between the trees, but we tried to keep the cattle grazing on the school meadow to save the others for our hay supply. During that summer, it became commonplace to see a bear or moose sharing the territory with the cattle. They were never a problem. We attributed it to the fact that there was plenty of food—gophers, willow, grass, and berries—for them all.

A year after we had moved to the ranch, in the early spring, Gordon had to make a trip to Whitehorse for some supplies. As I was expecting our second child in a month, Norma and I stayed alone at the ranch. I was fine during the day, but when it got dark, it was so quiet I could hear a pin drop inside the cabin. All the eerie sounds in the night were magnified.

I was doing dishes in the wash pan in front of the window—whistling bravely, when I heard a sound on the windowpane a foot from my nose. I looked up, startled, and stared right into the red-rimmed eyes of a ghost looking in the window! It had a long, skinny white head and huge, shiny black eyes rimmed with red. I stared in horror—frozen to the spot. It suddenly threw up its head and whinnied. I realized it was our old black horse with the white-blazed face. I had forgotten to feed him his nightly treat of oats.

When my nerves settled down again, I blew out the lights so things couldn't see inside, as we hadn't hung our curtains yet. I went to bed expecting that Gordon would be along soon.

I tossed and turned most of the night but fell into a troubled sleep just before daybreak. Suddenly, I was jerked awake by a loud, deafening SQUAWK right over my head. An old raven had landed on the roof! Totally unnerved, I got dressed and went outside into the sunshine, wiping the tears away.

At that moment, I heard a truck coming across the ice. It was Tis Evans, a friend of ours, and another fellow. They were coming from Atlin and just stopped by to see if there was anything we needed.

"Gordon's not back yet, so if you see him, please tell him to hurry, will you?" I asked them.

Tis Evans was a rough outdoors man, small and wiry, with a face burned black from the glare of the sun on the snow and weathered from long hours of facing the driving winds of the lake. He was shy around women, much preferring the company of a good bottle of overproof rum. I saw him glance at my large tummy; he must have noticed my red eyes, too. He sounded a bit embarrassed, but concerned.

"If you want to come in with us, we'd drive real careful." He looked so worried I had to smile.

"No, I'll be fine." I said. "You'll probably meet him on the lake, anyway."

As I watched them drive out of sight, I wished I had accepted the offer. Gordon got back that afternoon. He said that he had seen Tis, who told him he'd better get home, pronto!

On May 24, 1947, Kirk was born in the old General Hospital in Whitehorse. We had driven to town over the muddy road three days earlier. I had a much easier delivery this time.

We had wanted a son very much—now here he was. Our world had suddenly become richer.

As soon as we could leave the hospital, we were back at the ranch. Norma was as thrilled as we were with our new arrival.

Now she wasn't the only child on the ranch. She treated her little brother like a doll.

We were limited to the amount of hay that we could put up—some years were plentiful, of course, but other years the crop was scarce. We had a wild variety called blue-joint which was extremely nutritious. The animals thrived on it.

We had unlimited summer range for cattle, though. With the lake on one side of the meadows and steep mountains on the other, we had a natural enclosure that confined them. We had to whittle our herd down in the fall to fit the haystack, so to speak. It seemed like a practical plan to bring in some yearlings in the spring, to run with the established herd, fatten them up all summer, and butcher them in the fall. This plan turned out very well for us in the long run.

If we were to haul yearlings from Fort St. John and Dawson Creek, 900 miles along the Alaska Highway, we first had to build a road out to the main Tagish road. This we did without the convenience of a surveyor; it ended up being just ten miles long. So now the name Ten-Mile Ranch became doubly appropriate.

To do this, Gordon and a friend searched out the shortest and best route to take. They started at opposite ends to blaze the trees. Blazing means to cut short notches in the bark of trees to serve as markers. The two men actually met in the middle of the trail right on course.

We had a D-2 Cat which Gordon used for building the road. Then he pulled a drag over it made from steel crossbars. When this was finished, Gordon, Norma, and I picked rocks every time we went to Carcross and again on the way home. Before long, we had that road in good shape.

We then bought a bigger truck and started hauling young heifers from Fort St. John. With our original brood cows and their calves to guide them, the new stock settled in to graze and to put on weight. It seemed that the moment they were unloaded from the truck, they put their heads down and never lifted them all summer. In the fall, they were eighteen to twenty months old and had grown tremendously. This worked well financially, as we had no expenses except for the initial purchasing and hauling cost.

After the weather turned and it started to freeze at night, we'd begin butchering. Slaughterhouses were not a requirement yet. In fact, I believe we were one of three in the Yukon who were raising cattle. The folks at the Pelly Ranch, on the Yukon River 300 miles away, and Steve Veerman at Robson on the Carcross Road, also kept a few head.

The method we used was clean and efficient. Jock Milne always came to help with this job. He could drop the animal to be butchered with just one shot from the gun, killing it instantly, every time. This was done in a patch of trees that were padded underneath with clean pine needles and leaves. The animal was then hoisted up with a block and tackle that was attached to a strong limb and skinned and butchered right there. Next, they were hung in quarters in our screened-in meat house for a week to cure. The meat was then delivered to the customers, who had already put in orders for front or hind quarters. This was choice beef and in high demand. One of our main sales source was the Choutla Indian Residential School in Carcross.

There wasn't much at the ranch in the way of haying equipment, except for the old horse mower and a dump-rake. So Gordon purchased a gas tractor for $1,000 and used it to put up hay. He also built a trailer with a hay rack on it. We would hand-rake the hay into piles to dry, then fork it into the rack, which held about a ton of hay. Norma and I (and Kirk when he got old enough) would climb up and tramp it down to make room for more. It was hot, sweaty work, and the blackflies were sometimes out in full force; but we used insect repellant to hold them at bay. We worked up healthy appetites doing this, but we felt like a million. And when we were done, we'd bed down in the hay while Gordon drove us home to the hay shed. The scent from the fresh hay was wonderful. By the time we got there, we'd be sound asleep.

By 1948, we were in a new house at Ten-Mile. By then we had a large vegetable garden, which yielded more potatoes, carrots, turnips, lettuce, and cabbage than we could possibly use. The garden was planted in a spot where a large cattle barn had once been built. The soil was rich and compost-like in texture. We needed no fertilizer to grow first-class organic vegetables. Some of our heads of lettuce weighed four pounds apiece and the cabbage ten to twelve pounds. We kept enough to fill our root cellar and the *Tutshi* took the surplus. Planting and tending the garden was my job, during which I transplanted hundreds of bedding plants, all started from seed.

With choice cuts of our own beef, moose in the fall, fresh lake trout, grayling, and whitefish from the lake plus blue grouse and spruce hens and the odd mountain goat or sheep for variety, we lived like kings. There were also many wild berries close by, which I canned and made into jams and jellies.

It was a lot of work, though. We had no electricity those first years at the ranch, and no refrigeration. So I'd make garden-vegetable mustard pickles with baby onions, carrots, cauliflower, and cabbage. They were delicious. We'd also can moose meatballs, steaks in gravy, and trout fillets, in quart mason jars, which tasted just like choice salmon.

To do this, I had a wood-burning stove in the yard. I'd haul buckets of water from the lake to fill a round galvanized tub—the same tub we took our baths in. The stove had to be stoked continuously with wood until the water boiled. To ensure that the meat or fish would be safe to eat, the jars had to be kept covered with the boiling water for four hours. Doing large batches at a time helped make it worthwhile. Canning outside in the fresh air took away much of the drudgery, and it wasn't quite so far to carry the water.

Saving the Cattle

We got out of bed after the first big freeze, in November of 1948, and looked out the window to see a number of cows sliding around on the ice forty feet from shore. These were the cows left after the first butchering. We had brought them in from the meadow to the corral we had built close to our house and outer buildings, which by now included a hay shed and barn. Winter had arrived and we had to feed them hay and grain now. The corral gate had somehow swung open in the wind and the animals were out looking for water. Now they found themselves on the ice which had formed during the night. The ice was only four inches thick, and by the time we threw on our clothes, the cows had started falling through. Gordon fired a shot into the air to alert Mary Clancy, a neighbor, who came running minutes later.

We all grabbed axes, walked gingerly out to where the cows were, and began chopping channels through the ice toward shore. The biggest problem was trying not to chop their noses, as they would swim right up to the edge of the ice in their anxiety to get out.

Mary did clip one; it was just a small gash but it bled profusely, turning the almost blinding whiteness of the snow around the animal's head into a harsh red. I tried not to look in her direction, as nausea threatened to overcome me. I couldn't afford to be sick right then. We were all far too busy.

The temperature that morning was thirty degrees below zero but the furious chopping kept us from getting cold. Finally, we had them all out and herded into the barn.

One stupid animal kept running past the door and Gordon chased her around the barn a couple of times. He abruptly realized that the activity was probably doing her more good than being penned up inside. 'Maybe not so stupid after all,' he thought. After a while, the cow went inside on her own. Another one was pretty weak and just sagged to the ground after getting out of the water. We got a big robe and covered her up—all three of us massaging her until the circulation improved and she was strong enough to get up.

A close escape—we were lucky we'd saved them all. Another lesson learned—from now on we would keep them penned up until there was no question that the ice was thick enough to hold them.

More Memories

Sometimes, in the winter months, the snow would be too deep to use the road. If we wanted to go to Carcross, we were restricted to traveling over the ice on foot—using snowshoes if the snow hadn't packed yet. Fourteen miles seems like a long way now, but then we'd think nothing of hiking into town on special occasions, with a sleigh in tow.

I remember New Year's Eve in 1949. Gordon and I hiked to Carcross for the dance at the schoolhouse—it wasn't all work and no play. We left Norma and Kirk with our friend Mary Clancy—she who had helped rescue the cows from the ice—an Irish girl who had taken a year's sabbatical from teaching and had built herself a cabin at Ten-Mile, half a mile from ours. We danced until five in the morning, then a group of us went to a friend's house for breakfast. After that, we hiked the fourteen miles back home, slept a few hours, and felt great when we woke up.

Unlike many people at that time, we never had a dog team. Sometimes it was too cold to venture out on the ice at all. When the temperature dropped and the wind came up, all the clothes in the world couldn't keep you warm, it seemed.

Gordon often tells about traveling on the lake with a big man by the name of Geddes. He let Gordon mush his dog team while he rode in the sleigh. The man was constantly complaining about the bitter cold.

"I think I'm freezing to death," he kept saying.

Gordon finally said, "Why don't you try running behind for a while? Maybe you'd warm up."

"Me?" he replied in indignation. "I'd sooner stay here and freeze like a man than get off and run like a dog!"

Gordon built a nifty little playhouse for the kids. Norma was six now and Kirk two. He screened it in and painted the lower walls white and the roof red. We put a miniature potbellied heater inside (for show only) and lots of toys, mostly homemade. The mosquitoes were bad that year and we thought the kids would have more fun playing in there, instead of getting bitten up.

They spent most of the time, however, with their noses pressed up against the screen, yelling, "We want to come out!"

Oh well, we tried.

When I got my first gas washing machine—and could throw away the old scrub board—it was a happy day, indeed. We set up the washer outside because it was closer to the water supply—the lake. It had a kick start and a hand-operated wringer, and I thought it was wonderful. Later on, I even had a gas iron, with the little air pump on the fuel tank. It worked perfectly, although it used to scare me periodically by flaring up. For lights, we had Aladdin lamps plus the regular kerosene models. I wasn't overly fond of cleaning those darn lamp globes every day, but it was one more thing that had to be done.

One summer, an Indian family made a temporary wood camp a couple of miles down the lake. They had three boys and one girl. They lived on fish and whatever wildlife that was available in the vicinity.

The kids would occasionally venture over and unobtrusively hang around the edge of our yard, curious to see what was going on in our camp. They probably wanted to see what our kids were doing as well. We would encourage them by offering homemade cookies. After a while, they lost most of their shyness. One day the oldest boy, who was around ten years old, brought us some meat.

"My Dad hunt bear, he say you eat good."

"Tell your Dad thanks a lot," I told him. "We'll eat it tonight."

It was the leg of very young bear and just fit into my largest roaster. That night we had company for dinner. He was a young college student who had come down from the Yukon Experimental Farm which the government operated at Haines Junction, roughly 100 miles west of Whitehorse. He was there to check on the experimental plot that the superintendent had in our meadow. He was testing a small patch of ground with some grain seed for us. Gordon invited him to dinner before he went back to town. He sat down to sliced roast, mashed potatoes and gravy, cranberry sauce, and all the trimmings. He seemed to be really enjoying the meal.

As I passed the meat around for the third time, he said, "I think I will. Tell me, is that veal? It sure is good."

"No, that's a leg of bear," I told him. "Have you had it before?"

"You wouldn't be pulling my leg now, would you?" he ventured apprehensively.

"Of course not; we have it all the time," I lied.

"Oh, I didn't mean it wasn't good—I've had two helpings already, though. I don't think I have room for any more, really."

Something had changed his mind and I thought he looked embarrassed and a bit pale.

"Well, have some blueberry pie then."

"Sure wish I had enough room," he said. "Excuse me...."

With that, he hurried out the back door. When he came back, he was a shade paler yet, but acted as if nothing had happened.

"Just went to make sure I hadn't forgotten to bring along those progress forms," he said. "But they were in the glove compartment, thank goodness."

Some people sure have weak stomachs.

After the war, the S.S. *Tutshi* started running again, having been taken off the run while the U.S. Army was operating the railroad.

"Do you ever wish you were still a deckhand on that boat?" I asked Gordon one day.

"No. But those were good days, too," he answered.

He began reminiscing about his life back then, in his *Tutshi* days.

6

S.S. *Tutshi* and Ben-My-Chree

Flashback

Gordon had worked for the White Pass Transportation Company as deckhand on the S.S. *Tutshi* for five summers, from 1937 to 1941. This paddle wheeler had plied the waters of Tagish Lake since 1917, carrying freight and passengers from Carcross to various locations along the eighty-mile run. The company paid the deckhands two dollars a day, gave them board and room, plus return fare to Vancouver—if they stayed for the season. The boat ran every day from Carcross to Ben-My-Chree, the wilderness resort at the end of Tagish Lake. Passengers were thrilled with their twenty-one–hour lake trip and thoroughly enjoyed the dances that were held every night on deck. The deck covering was canvas. Part of Gordon's job was to keep it waxed so it would make a good surface to dance on. Of the thirty-two men on the crew, some doubled as a band that included a pianist, guitar player, and drummer. The crew had as much fun as the passengers.

"I'll bet you were glad you never learned to play a musical instrument," I teased Gordon. "That way you got to dance all night. What a job!"

The crew members consisted of captain, pilot, two mates, five deckhands, purser, four cooks, pantry man, seven stewards, and some extras. The *Tutshi's* crew included English waiters, for the service was first class. The boat handled 110 people. They left Carcross at twelve noon and arrived at Ben-My-Chree at seven o'clock in the evening. On the return run, they would tie up halfway, from midnight until six, at the Tutshi River, arriving in Carcross at nine in the morning. By noon, another load of passengers were boarding. Lunch, dinner, and breakfast the next morning were all included in the fare of fifteen dollars per person.

Among the celebrities taking the trip in Gordon's time were Robert Taylor and Clark Gable. Gordon said they were friendly, although reserved and didn't stand out from the rest of the passengers. The captain told them that there were a couple of boys on the crew who could tell them more than he could about the hunting business.

Scotia Mac, the Captain, made sure that Gordon and his friend, Archie, met Taylor and Gable because the two actors wanted to know about the wildlife in the area. They intended to come back on a hunting trip the next year. The four men had an enjoyable visit swapping moose stories. Gordon and Archie often went on hunts together, when their work was finished at the end of the season.

The history of Ben-My-Chree itself is fascinating. Otto Partridge was the first to discover the spot that he later named Ben-My-Chree (Manx Gaelic for "Girl of My Heart").

In 1897, he had come up from California to investigate the Klondike gold strike. Arriving at Lake Bennett, he became aware of a need for boats between Bennett and Whitehorse, so he seized the opportunity and founded the Lake Bennett and Klondike Navigation Company. He built three boats, the *Ora, Flora,* and *Nora.* These eighty-foot sternwheelers were named the Mosquito Fleet because of their size; they were the first ones in the country.

When the White Pass railway between Bennett and Whitehorse neared completion, the Partridges moved to Millhaven Bay on Lake Bennett. They ran a sawmill there with a partner named Ludwig Swanson for several years. When the Gold Rush began slowing down, there was no longer a great need for a sawmill; so the partners turned to mining ventures, staking claims where conditions looked interesting.

The Partridges were approached by prospector Stanley McLellan, who had found some promising gold showings in the area later known as Ben-My-Chree. He wanted them to engage in a mining operation with himself and his wife, Anne. Intrigued by the idea, Otto agreed. Before long, they had a project going which employed a dozen or so men. They started building a tramway up the mountain. All went well until a huge landslide struck on October 11, 1911, burying the mine and killing Stanley and Anne McLellan instantly.

The Partridges gave up mining at that point and put all their efforts into creating a superb English-style country garden. They built a cozy log home and turned it into a legendary wilderness wonderland.

Then the *Tutshi* started running to Ben-My-Chree and it became the fashionable spot for well-to-do tourists to visit. The White Pass offered some assistance to the Partridges in return for their hospitality and had Japanese gardeners brought in early in the spring to build greenhouses, start the bedding plants, and help with the many chores around the place.

Some of the early visitors included the Prince of Wales, President Roosevelt, and Lord Byng.

Kate presided as a gracious and elegant hostess—welcoming all the guests in formal gowns of velvet and lace and taking them to the drawing room where she sat at the organ and entertained. It was the same organ she had insisted on having carried over the rugged Chilkoot Trail (along with her best china, silver, and linen) when she hiked over it to join her husband, years before.

Kate could handle a rifle, trap, and hunt like a man, but she never forgot how to act like a lady. No wonder Otto called her "Girl of My Heart."

In the early days of its history, the *Tutshi* had been used to haul freight, mail, and passengers destined for Atlin, B.C. They were taken from Carcross to Taku Landing, where they were loaded onto the train that ran on the Taku Tramway, the shortest railroad in the world—two and a quarter miles long. The White Pass purchased it in 1900. It was complete with passenger cars, conductors, and locomotives. The Duchess, one of the original units, can still be seen on display at Carcross, beside the railway station. Cost for this trip was two dollars and if there was a heavy load, the passengers were asked to get off and push. This was the railway that Gordon and I rode on during our honeymoon.

It spanned the portage between Tagish and Atlin lakes dropping forty feet in two miles to Scotia Bay, on Atlin Lake. The S.S. *Teheran* would be waiting to be loaded with the freight and passengers, who were then transported to Atlin, B.C.

In 1936, the expense became too great for the White Pass Company to keep the *Teheran*, the large Atlin Inn which they also owned and operated, plus the railroad—all operating for such a short season. So the *Teheran* was hauled up on the beach in Atlin, the hotel was dismantled, and the railroad was restricted to carrying freight and mail only, Tuesdays and Thursdays.

At this time, the *Tutshi* began handling passengers only for the rest of its run on Tagish Lake.

Otto Partridge died in 1930 and the "girl of his heart" six months later. Their old partners, Ludwig Swanson and his wife, carried on running Ben-My-Chree, with the cooperation of the White Pass, in the same grand manner that the Partridges had run it. The Japanese gardeners still started plants early in the spring. They had cultivated over two acres of flower gardens by then. Some of the delphiniums grew to be eight to ten feet high and the pansies and poppies were five inches across. In the fertile glacial silt, the plants prospered beyond imagination. The tourists were certainly enthralled to see such a display in this remote place. Another attraction was the homemade rhubarb wine, aged to perfection in the wine cellar, some of it dating back to the Partridge days. The tradition of serving each tourist a small glass of the delicacy was preserved and it was sipped with pleasure. But it was now Mrs. Swanson who entertained them at the organ.

"I'll bet you never dreamed when you were working on the *Tutshi* that you'd be living here at Ten-Mile now, eight years later, supplying the boat with fish," I said.

Gordon had purchased a commercial fishing license and was now fishing for the paddle wheeler. He used four-inch gill nets; this way they never caught anything too small. He would anchor one end to the shore and the other end to a buoy. He'd run the nets every day, but leave them out a week or ten days at a time. To run them, he'd lay across the bow of the boat on his stomach so that he could lift the mesh up and take the fish out while pulling the boat along the net—dropping it behind him as he emptied it. When the fish were all out, he'd go back to the buoy and pull on the net to stretch the slack, readying it for the next catch. Sometimes the outer end would be in 100 feet of water with a long rope attached to it.

He caught a lot of trout, the largest weighing from thirty-five to forty pounds.

One year, Gordon's dad spent the summer with us. Being an avid fisherman, he would take the boat out and troll for trout with a steel line. Many days, he and Gordon would just take the net out of the water and get their quota for the *Tutshi* by trolling for the fish.

The tourist boat came by the ranch at the same time every day. They couldn't dock at our wharf because the water was too shallow; so they just cut the motors and slowed down while Gordon went out to meet them in the middle of the lake. Each day he would swing out with his eighteen-foot wooden boat, carrying 150 to 200 pounds of lake trout out to the *Tutshi*. There were gangway doors on the side above the water level and he'd throw the sacks up to the deckhands.

The passengers liked watching the fish being delivered fresh every day and they would hang over the deck railing to take pictures of the fisherman and of the little girl steering the boat. Norma was a real help to Gordon. She learned to handle the boat when she was six years old.

This lake trout was the specialty of the dining room and the tourists seemed to really enjoy it.

When we had guests on weekends at the ranch, as we very often did, we would have our own specialty of fish and chips, served with a fresh salad from the garden. We had a long picnic table outside with benches. Guests could eat to their hearts' content and would go home raving about the food. Often we would take them horseback riding after dinner. Many times, they would stay overnight in the guest cabin—our name for the hay shed. They would bed down in sleeping bags in the haystack, which made a lovely, soft, fragrant place to sleep.

Back To Town Again

Norma took her first two grades of schooling by correspondence. She thought it was fun and I enjoyed the experience of teaching her. She learned the lessons quickly and easily. Her reports came back with glowing comments. By the third grade, though, we thought it was time she had more competition and contact with kids her own age.

We realized we would have to move back to Carcross. We could still spend our weekends and holidays at the ranch, even though it would mean moving the livestock to Carcross, too, at least for the winter.

The year was 1950, and our second son, Ted, was on his way. Before we made the move back to Carcross, we would have to go in and make arrangements for a place to live.

We decided we'd build another house there that we could rent out at a later date, not wanting to evict the Nelson family from our old house. Not now, anyway, as the Nelsons were already thinking about moving back to Atlin, now that the road was completed; they just hadn't made up their minds as to when.

There had been a U.S. Army camp at Johnson's Crossing at Mile 834 on the Alaska Highway, built during the construction of a steel bridge over the Teslin River. The buildings had been turned over to Canadian War Assets when the project was finished. Now they were up for bid and we were able to buy a small building—about 12 x 14 feet—for twenty-five dollars. It had been used previously as a screened-in cooler. It was large enough to convert into a cottage by adding another room and a porch. We moved it onto a lot we had bought across the road from our original home, painted it, and put in cupboards and furniture— and it became livable and quite cozy.

Moving from the ranch back to Carcross was quite an undertaking. Our road was in traveling condition again, except for a swampy area on the edge of the meadow. We had to leave our pickup on the town side of the swamp and use the tractor for transportation to the ranch buildings. Gordon had made a trial run and decided we could manage a trip to town by strapping a horse saddle onto the cowling of the tractor for me to ride on, while he held the kids on his lap—a novel way to travel.

When it was time to go, we set off, having changed into our dress up clothes as we were going to have dinner with Aunt Maude and Uncle Emerson. By that time, they were living in the cabin they had built on Craig Lake, about eight miles out of Carcross on the Tagish road.

As we were driving through the swamp, a calamity occurred. I was sitting astride the saddle, clutching the horn with both hands and leaning a bit to the right so I wouldn't obstruct Gordon's view. Everything was going fine when suddenly, and without any warning, the cinch on the saddle came loose and I was literally thrown, as if from a horse, into that huge swamp-puddle. I landed flat on my back, the slimy mud oozing up all over and around me. More angry than hurt, I sat up and felt around blindly in the mud for my glasses, which had flown off somewhere. Miraculously, I found them—not even broken. Wiping them off the best I could, I looked up to see why help from above had not yet arrived. Still furious, I saw the children's frightened faces—they were almost in tears—and Gordon was trying to reassure them that I was okay.

Okay indeed!

There I sat in the mud—expecting a baby in four months— and he was comforting the kids!

Then, suddenly, I saw the humor of my ludicrous situation and started laughing. I laughed until my stomach ached. Everyone joined in and the seriousness of the episode was over.

We went back to the ranch to change my clothes and repair the cinch, then started out again. This time there were no mishaps.

We stopped at Aunt Maude's and had a delicious hot meal, topped off with her wonderful homemade ice cream, which, in those days, we ate in soup plates filled to the brim. I can still taste that ice cream in my mind. We made it the old-fashioned way in a wooden bucket that held a smaller metal container inside. The container had a paddle inside that stirred the ice cream until it was the right consistency for eating. We packed ice and rock salt all around the container. Uncle Emerson would throw a burlap sack over it and let the kids take turns sitting on this, to hold the ice down, while he turned the handle around. I wish I could remember that recipe.

Soon we were settled, although a bit crowded, in our new cottage. Gordon began looking for ways to supplement our now meager income. For a while, he bought and hauled packhorses from Fort St. John for an outfitter in Telegraph Creek, B.C.

95

Before long, our renters moved back to Atlin and we were able to return to our home again. I was very happy to be back there with lots of space and the beautiful view of the lake.

We excavated under the house to put in a well—the first one in town. We also bought a light plant and had our own electricity, which was another first for Carcross.

Bobby Robson and his wife were the hotel proprietors at this time. He asked us if we'd supply them with electrical power. We charged them five dollars a month. It wasn't too long, though, before he started grumbling about all the money he imagined we were making out of this. So Gordon suggested that he buy the plant from us and we'd buy our electricity from him, at the same rate we were charging. Bobby thought this was a great idea, so a deal was struck right there. We heard via the moccasin telegraph later that he guessed he hadn't been overcharged for the electricity after all.

We still kept the garden at Ten-Mile, attending to it and checking on the cattle on the weekends.

On August 3, 1950, our third child, Ted, was born in the Whitehorse hospital, another very special little boy.

We began to wonder if there was enough industry in this small town to make ends meet, or whether we'd be better off in the larger town of Whitehorse. We decided we'd play it by ear, both of us hoping we wouldn't have to move. One day, the folks in town held a meeting. It was decided to approach the Territorial Government for funds to put a wooden sidewalk along the row of houses on the beach—the main street of town, actually. Until now, everyone had to walk along the road, over the sand and pebbles. The department of highways agreed to pay for the lumber, if we would build it ourselves. Everyone agreed to this wholeheartedly. It would be a community effort. We'd all pitch in and help each other. When the lumber arrived, everyone turned up in full force to begin the job of constructing the sidewalk.

As the days went by, and the project started taking shape, the number of crew members began to decrease. One morning, Gordon walked down the street to where they'd left off the night before, noticing there was one less helper than there had been the day before.

96

"What do you suppose is happening here, Alf?" he asked the old fellow who was hammering in nails.

Alf Dixon looked up from his work, pushed his cap up, and said, "You know what these bastards are doing, don't you? They're all dropping out as soon as we go past their cabins!"

"Well, we've got a ways to go yet," replied Gordon.

The work continued on and by nightfall they were just beyond Dixon's house, making pretty good progress. The next morning, Alf was missing.

To make a long story short, by the time they had reached our house on the end, Gordon had to hire Frankie Grant, one of the minister's sons, to help finish the sidewalk: Gordon's reward for helping from the start of the project but living at the end of the street.

Herman and Doris Peterson had been renting one of Matthew Watson's cabins along the row. They now decided to build themselves a home on the west side of ours. So we no longer had the house on the end.

Herman was a pilot for Northern Airways, the company that was owned and operated by George Simmons. Having no children, Doris was alone a lot while her husband was away flying. One day she came up with the idea of starting a small grocery store.

"I know there's room for another one in town and it would be a great way to use some of the produce you two grow on your ranch," she said. "I'll run it—the rest of you are so busy—and I need something to do."

The little building we had brought from Johnson's Crossing was empty now. With a little persuasion, Gordon and Herman decided to turn it into a small grocery store and to go into partnership, provided that Doris and I would look after it.

We all made a modest profit from our little business venture. Gordon and I supplied the building and fresh vegetables from the ranch. Our venture turned out to be short-lived, though, due to a change in circumstances.

The road to Atlin had been completed the previous year. George Simmons came to the decision that there was no longer enough business for Northern Airways to operate. He sold all his planes and began trucking the mail and freight to Atlin instead of flying it in.

Herman knew he would have to do something else now and he could visualize an opportunity in Atlin. We wished him and Doris luck as they left Carcross to start their own flying business. Herman turned out to be very successful in this enterprise.

Matthew Watson, the general store owner, quickly offered to buy out our stock when he heard the news, so we sold it to him. He probably wasn't a bit sorry to see the end of the competition, having had a monopoly since the early 1900s. The townsfolk were not too happy to see us close our doors, though, as the groceries quickly returned to their former prices. We converted the building back to a cottage and were lucky enough to rent it to the new schoolteacher and his wife right away.

That fall, in 1950, George Simmons came to see Gordon. He asked Gordon if he would like to do the mail and freight hauling from Carcross to Atlin. Gordon accepted his offer, as it was only two days a week and he figured he could fit it in between his other projects.

In 1951, we built three more cabins on the property across the road from our house, next to the cottage, and rented them all for the summer months.

Norma was going to school in the one-room schoolhouse close to home and loved it. At four years old, Kirk began to think he was really missing out on something good, and day after day would try to join the kids when they lined up to go into school.

"You aren't old enough yet," I told him. "Your time will come."

One day the teacher lined the kids up outside as usual and was calling them into the classroom single file when she noticed a little boy crawling in between the kids on his hands and knees. He had hoped he wouldn't be noticed. When he found out it didn't work, he stamped his feet and grumbled all the way home. Nice if this attitude could have lasted throughout his teenage years! Once again, after he'd been chased away from the school door, Kirk vented his frustration by throwing rocks onto the roof of an elderly bachelor who lived close to us. The old fellow charged out and grabbed him by the scruff of the neck.

"What's going on here, you young scamp? I'm going to warm the seat of your trousers good!"

"Let me go! Let me go!" Kirk hollered. "I'll tell my Dad and he'll put tin ears on you!"

Whenever the kids acted up, Gordon used that expression to scare them into behaving. The neighbors' kids would stare, wide-eyed in awe, as they watched Kirk or Norma being scolded by their Dad.

"You be good or I'll put tin ears on you!" he'd say, and their hands would involuntarily go up to cover their ears.

We had plenty of space for building corrals on the sand dunes on the west end of town near our home. Each fall, we herded the cattle to Carcross with our horse Sister along the old telegraph line by the lakeshore for fourteen miles. It was always a chore, as much of the trail had become overgrown with willow or was blocked by windfall over the years since the trail had been used. In the spring, we'd take them back to the ranch.

Our kids started off trying to ride the steers we were raising for beef cattle, so their dad decided it was time they had ponies of their own. In the spring of 1952, he brought three Shetlands home from Fort St. John as well as the yearling steers. He dropped the steers off at the ranch to graze with the brood cows for the summer and unloaded the ponies in Carcross. So now the kids could ride on the beach and around the trails close to town.

Not long after this, Gordon had a chance to haul three loads of packhorses for an outfitter in Telegraph Creek. The horses were bought in Fort St. John, again, from Warne McKenzie, who soon became a very good friend of ours.

Warne was a real horseman. He talked, breathed, and lived horses and had bought and sold them all of his life. Our purchases over the years in both cattle and horses were done through Warne. Like everyone in the Fort St. John and Dawson Creek area, we trusted him implicitly.

One summer in 1953, Warne and his son Jimmy came to help us build more corrals and to put in a well and pump inside the fenced-in area. This would eliminate the need to drive the cattle down to the lake for water in the winter. Warne drove into the yard while work was in progress and to Norma's delight there was a beautiful little black mare in the back of the truck for her to break and ride herself.

By the age of ten, Norma was handling horses without any trouble. This was the thing she liked to do most of all and she put a lot of time and patience into training them. First she'd get them used to the saddle blanket by flipping it on and off their backs. Then she'd patiently lead them around and around with the saddle on. By the time she finally climbed into the saddle, they were so used to being handled that all they'd do was flinch a bit; they never did get around to bucking—usually. Norma named her mare Lady. The first time she tried to ride her, I watched with my heart in my mouth as she was thrown high into the air. She did a complete somersault and landed on her rear end—fortunately. She persevered, though, and soon had the mare acting like a lady—but only for her. Otherwise, Lady remained skittish and unpredictable; so, before long, we sold her to an outfitter.

Lady was the start of a long procession of horses we bought and sold over the next few years, the most memorable and loved ones being Tillicum, Echo, Chocolate, and Snake.

Tillicum was the oldest. He was a gentle pinto gelding who would stop immediately if one of the kids fell off and would not move until they got back on. He loved to run, but could be controlled with the slightest pressure of the reins. He had one bad habit: once his bridle was removed and he was set free, he was very difficult to catch again. We would sometimes chase him for an hour while he kept just an arm's length ahead of us. This was really hard to understand, as he became a lamb the minute you laid a hand on him. I often wondered if it was a game he liked to play; but it could certainly be annoying and frustrating when you were ready to go riding.

Echo was a big mare. She was a shiny black beauty—dependable, young, and much smoother to ride than Tillicum—but a lot less energetic.

Snake, a chestnut, was my horse. She combined all the good qualities of the other two. She had a habit, though, of wanting to veer off the trail if you didn't keep a tighter rein on the left side than the right. Given her head, she'd start going in a circle every time. Even Warne couldn't figure that one out—and he was supposed to be the expert on horses. Who can read their minds, though? Snake's first colt was a lovely little dark brown stud; we named him Chocolate. After that, she kept producing perfect colts every year.

The kids and I loved to race the horses on the wet, firmly packed sand on the beach, especially when the water level was low in the spring. On hot summer days after a long ride, we'd come home dusty and perspiring, get a bar of soap from the house, and ride the horses out into the lake where we'd all cool off. We'd wash the horses and sometimes our jeans (which we were still wearing). Then we'd set the horses free—while we rested on the beach and let the sun dry us off.

The Sawmill

It was during this time, in 1953, that the White Pass put in a creosoting plant in Carcross. Now they were looking for a source of railroad ties that would be reasonably close by. They gave Gordon the contract, largely because he had already scouted out all the timbered areas around there when he had had the pole contract. He also had a truck available in Carcross for the job. It was his largest enterprise and the most profitable one during the rest of the 1950s.

I really thought he was keeping busy enough as it was, but, as he pointed out, the cost of raising a family was increasing all the time. The various other jobs he had created for himself were actually a series of sidelines; it took all of them to make a decent living. It would be nice now to have one solid project to concentrate on again and it looked like this contract would be it. He decided that by hiring a small, competent crew, he could do the job and still maintain the ranch and livestock.

But first, we had to purchase a small sawmill to side the logs on four sides and cut them into six-and-a-half-foot lengths to make ties. And, we had to get a timber permit. Armed with a starter contract from J. C. Hoyt, superintendent of the White Pass and Yukon Route, for 10,000 ties at a dollar fifty-three each, Gordon began setting up the mill a few miles from Carcross on the Tagish road.

101

Warne stayed on to help out. Gordon also needed a sawyer to work on the mill. Someone suggested a fellow whom I will call Hank, who was supposed to be a man of considerable experience in this field.

Apparently he had been cutting trees up north, near the Alaska border, for a mill that had recently shut down. Hank was using a big old raw-boned horse to skid the logs out of the bush. Being short of hay, he would coax the horse along on a diet of a little hay supplemented with willow, poplar leaves, and whatever else was available. He agreed to come to work, but only if he could bring his horse along. No horse—no sawyer; so Gordon had to go up and haul them both back in his truck. He had misgivings at the time, because of the conditions he found them in.

Hank had slapped up a would-be barn or shed for his horse, out of slabs from the mill, but when the weather turned cold, being a kind-hearted fellow, he worried about keeping her warm enough. So, he tunneled in under the shed and lowered a barrel wood heater into the hole. When he fired it up, the heat from this stove, plus the horse, plus the manure (which never got shoveled out) made it very warm and steamy in the barn.

Hank's tent, on the other hand, was quite cold. Coming back to it after a days work was not very pleasant, so he moved in with the horse until the cold snap past. He rolled out his sleeping bag beside the horse and slept, seemingly oblivious to the fumes of ammonia that permeated the cramped quarters. He appeared to be right at home.

Gordon and Warne loaded the horse into the back of the truck. On the way back, Warne glanced out the back window.

"By God," he said, "I've hauled a lot of horses in my day, but that's the first one I've seen sitting up like a dog!"

The old mare was getting arthritic in the hind quarters and she had settled down into a sitting position to cope with the vibration of the truck.

We used to call Hank the first hippie in the Yukon because he had long, bushy gray hair down to his shoulders and an equally bushy gray beard. He turned out to be fairly capable at his job, however, in spite of being a rather wild looking character. He was half smart in some ways, but had strange and irrational ideas about other things. He was very good-natured, though. He saw a funny side to things that most other people couldn't see and would throw back his head and laugh hilariously.

Hank pitched his tent near the sawmill, which was about twelve miles from Carcross. He preferred this to staying in the trailer with the other men.

Hank liked most people and got along with the work crew, but every once in a while he would develop a grudge against someone in town. Then he'd put a hex, or what he called the evil eye, on him. He was convinced that this curse would do that person in eventually. Far from being bitter, the thought gave him much pleasure and he'd laugh with great glee at the fate that awaited the man or woman he had targeted. It would usually be someone who, in Hank's view, had committed a crime against the laws of nature. He would generally forget all about it after a few days.

He didn't like affluence of any sort; any form of luxury was a sin in his eyes. Hank was also a health-food fan long before it became so popular. He would extol the virtues of pumpernickel bread to anyone who would listen.

One day Warne McKenzie said to him, "Okay Hank, if it's so wonderful, why don't you bake some?"

"Sure, if you want me to," said Hank.

Gordon happened to be away in town that afternoon, so when Warne and the others left for work after lunch, Hank stayed behind to bake the bread.

Warne told us later that when the crew arrived back home for dinner, Hank was hard at work. He'd taken off his shirt, as it was hot in the kitchen, and was kneading away at the bread dough—in his grimy winter underwear. (He took a bath once a year, Gordon used to say, whether he needed it or not.) His hair, as usual, was still full of sawdust and pine needles from work and the heat was making the sweat run down his forehead in little globules, which picked up the dirt from his face on its way down before it dripped into the big pan of dough.

Warne sat back watching him for a while. Being a great one for getting some fun started, he began cracking jokes. He kidded poor Hank until he really had him going—and this, of course, caused Hank to sweat more profusely than ever. He'd laugh and shake his head, sending down a shower of dust and twigs from his hair. Then he'd reach inside his itchy underwear to scratch. With his fingernails black with hair and grime, back he'd go into the bread dough to knead some more. Gordon returned from town as the bread was coming out of the oven. It actually looked quite good after the baking. Hank couldn't understand why no one was hungry enough to eat one bite of his pumpernickel bread. It didn't go to waste, though. Between him and the horse, every last morsel was devoured and enjoyed.

The next time Gordon had to be away, Hank decided the propane stove would have to go. They were getting too modern at the mill—and to him this was not right or natural. He carried it outside and threw it over the bank. No luxuries around this camp was his reasoning. He brought in an old wood stove and set that up instead. Then he went out and brought in a bunch of scrap wood and bark, which he threw on the floor over the new linoleum.

Inviting Hank into the kitchen to bake pumpernickel had been a mistake; he now had a sort of proprietary attitude toward it. When Gordon came back and saw what had happened, he was mortified, to say the least. He and Warne took pride in keeping the trailer clean and neat. He decided it was time for Hank to go. He persuaded him that there was far more opportunity in Whitehorse for a man of his caliber. Hank cheerfully agreed.

Gordon hired a man called Two-man Macdonald for his next sawyer, so called because he could do the work of two men in one shift. This man stayed on as long as we kept the mill.

I kept busy at home all this time, getting the kids off to school and preparing meals. Gordon usually arrived home around six for dinner. The kids and I looked after the saddle horses and when Gordon was busy elsewhere, we'd feed and water the cattle as well. To water them in the winter months (before we put in the well and pump), we would drive them down to the lake, chop a hole in the ice, and let them drink, then take them back.

Before the well, everyone in the village had to get their water in buckets from the lake. The first person there in the morning would have to chop the hole. There was a joke in town—usually true—that each day many faces would be looking out of windows waiting for someone else to get her first bucket of water so they wouldn't have to do the chopping.

Jock Milne

One day we were feeding the cattle in the corral when a strange thing happened. One of our old brood cows suddenly stopped eating and, for no reason that we could see, began to stare intently over the top pole of the corral. Now this cow, which we had had for years, was always placid, easy to handle; she produced a fine calf faithfully every spring. But this day, she became more agitated and strained her neck to see better. Her eyes almost bulged out of her head. This behavior was so uncharacteristic that I walked around a barrel that was obstructing my view to see what was going on.

Down the road I saw Jock Milne. He was in town for the day on one of his rare trips from Tagish to get supplies. As he came closer, the old cow let out a bellow and leaped over the fence, clearing it by at least a foot. She had never jumped a fence in her entire life! She ran in terror down the beach, away from Jock. It looked so comical that Norma and I almost collapsed in laughter.

The only thing we could attribute her behavior to was the fact that Jock Milne used to help us butcher in the fall, at Ten-Mile. Jock had not been anywhere near the cattle for at least three years, but evidently the cow recognized him.

My Post Office

The last thing I ever expected to be was a postmistress. When Mrs. Rose, who had done the job in Carcross for twenty-five years, suggested that I take the job as she was retiring, I didn't take her seriously. She was quite persuasive, though, and insisted that I would be foolish to turn it down.

I began to think, 'Why not?' I knew that I would be taking on two jobs, actually: postmistress and janitor. 'Mrs. Rose has done it all those years,' I thought. 'Why couldn't I?'

I accepted the job and Mrs. Rose began training me in the various chores of filling out forms, ordering stamps and supplies, keeping records, and balancing the books every day. The cash was sent to Whitehorse in a registered package on mail days. The mail came in twice a week by train. Besides the local population of 120, there were the section crews at various points on the railway, the crew from the *Tutshi,* the village of Tagish (twenty miles away), and the people along the lake, all getting their mail through the Carcross Post Office. So there was enough business to keep the job interesting.

I was allowed one helper during the Christmas rush, but the rest of the time I was alone. Mrs. Rose had been right; I did enjoy the work. The post office was a pleasant change from the routine of keeping house. It was also nice to have a paycheck coming in every month. With the first one, I bought a portable typewriter and taught myself to type, as there was spare time between mail days. I bought a typing instruction book and covered the keys so that I couldn't peek. It gave me a feeling of real accomplishment. A year or two later, the department sent me an adding machine, so I no longer had to add the long columns in my head, although by this time I was getting very fast at it. This adding machine and my own typewriter represented the only office equipment I had, apart from the scales for weighing the parcels and larger letters.

I sent a requisition to the government to have the building painted. To my surprise, they contracted the job out that same summer. After that, I took a real pride in keeping the office spotless and running smoothly. It became my own little oasis and I enjoyed visiting with everyone in town when they came for their mail. I ran the post office for five years, from 1955 to 1960.

We had settled into the normal routine of life in a small town. When Norma was fourteen years old, in 1957, she had to go to Whitehorse to school, as the eighth grade was the highest available in Carcross.

The government was not nearly as flush with family assistance for education (or anything else, actually) in those days. We were totally responsible for the cost of transportation to school for our kids, as well as their board and room. Day care, of course, had never even been thought of yet, certainly not in mixed company. It was probably taking seed in a great many mothers' minds at the time, however.

So Norma went to live with Gordon's brother and his wife in Whitehorse during the week. We would pick her up or she'd catch a ride home with another student on the weekends.

She and her girl friends were in the midst of the Elvis Presley craze and many an evening our living room was converted into a dance hall, while the girls jived and twisted to the popular rock and roll. They loved it when I'd join in at the ripe old age of thirty-two. Sometimes we'd even get Gordon rocking to the music.

7

Dezadeash Lodge

The cattle still grazed every summer at Ten-Mile, but in 1959 we'd had an exceptionally dry season and our hay crop would have to be supplemented if we were going to keep the breeding stock in Carcross over winter. The closest hay source was 185 miles north of us, on a meadow at Dezadeash Lake.

Gordon and I set off from Carcross in our flat-decked truck with the hay rack on it to buy a load of hay from Bun Beloud. It was the first time I had been in this part of the country.

So this was the Dezadeash area. It was hard to visualize this peaceful setting as the same place that had been the scene of a terrible massacre by the White River Indians so many years ago. The Klukshu tribe was the loser in that war. There was only one survivor, a young girl.

Bun said he'd drive us down the road about seven miles to see if we could get a salmon to take home with us from the Indians who had a camp there. Coming into the small smoky village of Klukshu, we could see rows and rows of salmon strips hanging on drying racks; small bonfires were burning under each one, sending up columns of smoke, which not only gave the fish its flavor but also cured it for keeping purposes.

"Do you eat it, too?" I asked an old woman who was poking up one of the fires.

"Sure," she said. "You try it. Here."

She handed me a strip of salmon. In order not to offend anyone, I had to take a chew. To my surprise, it wasn't bad at all. A couple of Indian women were sitting on a bench outside a log cabin, doing their beadwork on some moccasins. It was beautiful work, and before we left there I had bought moccasins for each of the kids, and a pair of slippers for myself. Then we went back to the lodge for dinner.

Bun Beloud had been a trapper and prospector in that area before the Alaska Highway and the Haines Road were completed, in 1942.

The U.S. Army had had a maintenance camp at Mile 125 on the Haines Road, close to the shore of Dezadeash Lake. It was 125 miles north of Haines and 135 miles west of Whitehorse. When the army moved out, it declared the buildings to be surplus, so Bun bought the ones he needed through Canadian War Assets.

He bought the campsite from the territorial government, and built a lodge there. He installed a gas pump, a garage for servicing trucks, and a bunkhouse for the truckers. He and his family ran the lodge for eighteen years; it was called Beloud Post.

The Belouds were true pioneers in that part of the world. Bun had a stocky build, and a tough manner that couldn't quite hide the twinkle in his intensely blue eyes. He was quite vocal, and a bit opinionated, which was characteristic of a lot of Yukon sourdoughs. His wife was a rather thin little woman, very enthusiastic, who got along well with people. She was an avid reader of books, and was famous for her homemade cake doughnuts, of which she kept an unending supply in gallon jars in the kitchen.

Bun had staked 120 acres of meadow land, across the road and a quarter mile south of the lodge, and was able to obtain it later for a minimal amount of money. Bun had been putting up hay there for years, placing a large haystack right in the middle of the meadow. He was forever having to chase the moose away from this hay, not having a fence to keep them out. There was an old rotary horse-baler there but he was just piling the hay into a large stack with his little farm tractor, rake, and mower.

After we had enjoyed a delicious meal and finished it off with coffee and Mrs. Beloud's doughnuts, we went down to the meadow with Bun to pick up our hay.

It was nighttime by now but the ground was covered with a light fall of snow and it was quite bright under a full moon. I had never seen a prettier setting. The mountains are very high, and close. Surrounded on all sides by this snow-capped magnificence nestled the hay meadow, brilliant and sparkling with ice crystals on the snow in the moonlight.

"If I could have one wish, it would be to have a home right here in the middle of this meadow; right where Bun has his haystack," I told Gordon.

It sounds almost unbelievable, but that's exactly what I had a few years from then.

One day, after this trip for hay, we were in Whitehorse shopping when we ran across Bun standing on a street corner. We stopped to talk to him.

"Do you want to buy a lodge?" he asked "I've decided to sell out; getting too old for this game."

We were taken by surprise, as we didn't even considered the possibility. Bun was determined to sell, though. Whenever we saw him in town after that, he would try to convince us that we were missing out on something good by not purchasing the lodge. And sure enough, the longer Gordon thought about it, the more appealing the idea seemed to be; then the time came, in 1960, when he decided that this was going to be our next move.

It was a very big decision to make, as it meant uprooting our entire lives, selling our ranch at Ten-Mile, our house and all the buildings at Carcross, our cattle—everything. It also meant I would have to give up the post office—and take our children out of school. Norma was already staying with people in Whitehorse and going to high school, but the two boys would have to take correspondence. We had no experience whatsoever in running a lodge or dealing with the general public in that type of enterprise.

For the first time in our married life, I had a severe attack of cold feet. Did I really want to disrupt our life like this—give up our home in that beautiful, picturesque setting on the beach of Lake Bennett? What did I know about managing a staff—or ordering supplies for an unknown number of people we'd be feeding in the cafe? Handling a payroll? The more I thought about it, the larger loomed the hurdles we would have to face.

'Pull yourself together,' I told myself severely. 'Where is your sense of humor anyway? You've never been afraid of challenges before have you?' I decided I'd just quit thinking about it, and get down to the chore of packing. Oh! The packing!

We had accumulated an incredible amount of things in eighteen years. Gordon had to leave me with most of it, as he was busy with the business end of things, plus hauling loads of equipment and paraphernalia to Dezadeash and bringing out truckloads of things from Ten-Mile.

When I found out we were getting the hay meadow with the lodge deal, I felt better about it; little did I realize it would be eight years before I'd have time to enjoy it, though.

I notified the Post Office Department that I was leaving, and began training a good friend of mine, Lillian Bear, who had applied for the job and been accepted. I was going to miss it. Gordon arrived home from one of his trips to Dezadeash one afternoon and asked me to get my coat on.

"I'm going to have to go right back. They're very busy at the lodge, and short-handed right now, so they need us badly." What I needed badly was a rest. I had put in an especially busy day at the office and gone home to dive right back into the packing. But I threw some things into a bag, and off we went, on the *very long* 185-mile drive.

Four hours later, we arrived. Gordon had not been exaggerating. The cafe was full; the dishes were piled high in the kitchen. I paused just long enough to roll up my sleeves. For the next two hours, I was deep into soapy dish water. The girl they had hired for this job had gone to the Junction and never bothered coming back.

This was my initiation into the lodge business.

The Belouds offered to stay and look after things until we were finished hauling our belongings and had our bearings.

The folks in Carcross put on a big going-away party for us in the community hall, and the next day, dragging my feet all the way and with a big lump in my throat, we pulled out of town. It would be quite a while before we went back for a visit.

There were thirteen horses by now in our family, and rather than listen to the laments of the kids and myself, Gordon agreed to haul them to Dezadeash.

Let me take you on a verbal guided tour of the buildings at Dezadeash, as they were when we first bought them.

The lodge was a long building with a lobby at both ends. On the walls hung lynx, wolverine, and bear skins. The place had a rustic charm all of its own, and it was tempting to leave it like that;

but we had come at a time when the public was demanding modern, functional accommodation, and we knew we'd have to rebuild.

One of the lobbies held the office, the other lounge chairs and bookshelves. The guest rooms and two large bathrooms were located in the middle, the doors opening onto both sides of a long hallway. Walking straight through the office lobby, you would come into the dining room, which had one large table and wooden benches on each side, and just beyond this was a large kitchen that had a heavy-duty army cookstove with a grill on top. The walls were lined with deep shelves, from the floor to the ceiling, one set holding canned goods, the other dishes and cooking utensils. The far end of the kitchen was used as a laundry room, as there was so much space. This corner was equipped with a commercial-sized agitator washing machine with wringer rollers, and next to it a mangle for ironing sheets, (this was before permapress was available). The back door of this room led outside to the rows of clotheslines and to the wonderful walk-in cooler with a large freezer compartment in one end.

There was a big old garage to the north of the lodge, which served as a service station and where the tires, parts, and equipment were kept. The light plant, our only source of electricity, was also kept there. In front of the cafe was an old-fashioned, hand-operated gas pump, which we immediately replaced with a modern one.

When we first arrived, the first busy spell of the season had just started, and the Belouds hadn't taken on their full summer staff yet. Knowing that we were coming to take over shortly, they had wanted us to have an input into the hiring. They did have the two girls from Australia, Doreen and Nonie, however, and an Indian girl, Mary Smith, who turned out to be an excellent and dependable employee for many years to come.

Doreen and Nonie's time in Canada was almost up. They had been with the Belouds all winter, and soon it would be time to fly home. The two of them had become like family members during their stay. To our delight, they agreed to stay on for another month. I really don't know how I'd have coped without those girls when the Belouds left, about a week after we got there. They had received training in lodge work in their own country and were a fountain of knowledge to me. I wanted to learn every aspect of the many jobs required to operate the business, and they were willing and most helpful.

They taught me the correct way to fold and stack sheets, how to operate the mangle, make up the beds with hospital corners, and many other things. I learned how to make up meal sheets for the government road crews to sign so I could send in the bill at the end of their stay with us. I learned how to order enough, but not too much, food to last at least two weeks, as we tried not to go into Whitehorse, a 268-mile return trip with the truck, any oftener than that. I learned to wait table, how to do fast-order cooking on the grill, how to make great quantities of soup, chili, pies, pancakes—everything. I wanted to know what to expect from our summer staff, when they arrived, and also how to take over for them on their days off.

'Once we have our full staff,' I thought, with the innocence of inexperience, 'it will be a snap.'

The summer's tourist rush seemed to hit us all at once. We still had our road crew of about eight men for breakfast and dinner, and lunches to make up every day. We also started getting two scheduled busloads of tourists, one every morning for coffee and doughnuts, and one in the afternoon for a full-course meal. On top of this, there were the drive-by tourists, stopping to gas up, get a tire fixed, have a meal, or get a room for the night.

Doreen, Nonie, and the Belouds had all left by then, and our kitchen staff eventually consisted of two cooks, two waitresses, a dishwasher, and Mary, our chambermaid. I worked for each one of them on their days off, took over when someone wasn't well, and most of the time I had to look after the bar as well, unless I could talk someone else into the job.

Our staff, of course, had to live in, as there were no other facilities close by. We did have a comfortable little staff cabin out behind the cafe, where the girls slept, but it still meant cooking a lot of extra meals, and doing more laundry.

I inherited the job of doing up the payroll—deducting income tax and vacation pay, figuring out their sick leave, and putting stamps in their unemployment insurance books (remember those stamps?)—besides doing our own daily book work and balancing both the cash register in the cafe and the one in the lounge every night. In my spare time, I tried to help the boys with their correspondence.

We had taken on quite an undertaking.

Gordon, along with our boys and a young Indian fellow, pumped gas, fixed tires, serviced the light plant, and took out fishing parties. Gordon also put up hay in the fall, which we sold right on the meadow to outfitters, game guides, and to some horse owners from Alaska.

The work load was becoming too much for me, finally, and we considered getting another girl; until I realized I'd just have one more person to spell off. What we needed was one spell-off person for the kitchen staff. We found a girl who was willing to take on this job and life became much easier—only a ten-hour day now instead of sixteen.

'Thank God, it's only seasonal,' I thought.

This is just an overview of our first summer at Dezadeash. The next year we remodeled the lodge throughout, tearing out the front wall and replacing the rental rooms with modern ones equipped with individual bathrooms and outside entrances. We built a walkway along the front, giving the front of the building a whole new look. We also put in a laundry room with automatic washers and dryers. The place was beginning to take shape.

Busy Days

Owning the lodge, Gordon used to say, was almost like being the managers of a small town. To begin with, there were all the buildings—cafe, cocktail lounge, garage, gas pumps, accommodation (we had twenty-two rooms in the lodge before we were done). We had our own power plant, our own sewer and water system, a transportation system (hauling our supplies from town), and we did all our own maintenance (a service man would have to travel almost 300 miles, return trip, from Whitehorse). We supplied our own wood for the furnaces that we used for the central heating system in the lodge and cafe. We also provided employment for between ten and thirteen people every summer.

114

For the first couple of years at the lodge, we were almost forced to close up and move to town in the winter months, as there was no maintenance on the road. But then Gordon picked up a contract with the Department of Transportation in Whitehorse, using his Cat for various jobs, including snow removal. I worked at the post office in Whitehorse during the Christmas rush the first year, and during the second winter I took a job with Hougen's Department Store, as office secretary.

In March, the government road crews would start opening up the Haines road, starting at the little town of Haines Junction and working south toward Haines, Alaska. When the thirty-four miles to our lodge was cleared of enough snow to make it passable, we would follow them out and shovel a path to the door—through what was quite often ten-foot drifts of snow. Then we'd fire up the furnace. The crew would move in, and we'd be in business once again.

We'd take Mary with us to help with the dishes and laundry, and the two of us managed fine in the old kitchen in the lodge. We would hang the sheets outside where they would freeze solid, then bring them in to hang on temporary clotheslines strung up in the hallway until they were dry.

We fed the crew family style, and when they were finished eating, they'd bring their dishes to the sink, sometimes even helping to dry them. They worked on the road from our place, going in both directions. When they had it cleared to the maintenance camp at 95 Mile, usually in about two or three weeks, they would move into the camp there. When the road crew left, there was always a quiet period at the lodge, until the road was cleared all the way to Haines.

We took advantage of this time to open up the cafe building again for the summer and prepare for the tourist rush that would come soon. Periodically during the summer, as work was needed on the road closer to the lodge, the crew would be back to stay again. This was good business, and we knew in advance exactly how many meals to prepare.

We were already getting business from Haines Junction by April—people coming out for a meal or to spend an evening in the lounge. This would sometimes turn out to be the busiest time of all for me, as Mary was our only help before we hired on a full staff, and there were many times when we'd have an unexpected rush that would keep us running for a few hours. Since this was a seasonal business, we usually had to find new staff members every year. There were exceptions to this, however. The girls we hired were university students from B.C. or Alberta usually, and this arrangement worked very well. Some of these girls liked it so well that they'd phone the next spring wanting to come back. And, in nearly every case, we were delighted to have them again. With cooks, it was a little more difficult, and although we had our good years (some of them were great), other years would be nightmares. But more about cooks later.

With the advent of the Alaska State Ferries, the traffic doubled, and the road was kept open year-round. We discovered it still didn't pay us to keep the lodge open in the winter months, however, after trying it for a year or two. We had a couple run it for us one winter, but this didn't work out very well, either, so from then on we just drained the water system and closed everything down until spring.

The ferry passengers arrived in Haines late in the afternoon, and about four hours after that we had a rush of traffic at the lodge. We could be partially prepared for the influx, but there were always people who liked to take in the sights of Haines before hitting the road and, generally, they would arrive when the staff was off for the night. This would leave me to look after the customers alone, as we only had two shifts in the cafe, one from 6:00 A.M. to 2:00 P.M. and the other from 2:00 to 10:00 P.M.

Gordon would be busy at the gas pump while I tried to pour drinks in the lounge, grill steaks in the kitchen, and rent rooms all at the same time. After a while, I became quite proficient at all this, even enjoying it when I wasn't too tired. Many of the people who stopped by were a pleasure to wait on, and we met many very interesting people, and made a lot of friends in the years we had the lodge.

We were fortunate to attract a group of repeat customers, who looked forward to a week or two of fishing every summer. Dezadeash Lake was exceptionally good for large lake trout. These sports fishermen also kept us supplied with fish for the cafe, as they always caught more than they could use. Our specialty on the menu was lake trout, and besides being popular, it was all profit for us. The bus drivers were very cooperative, and would phone us when they got as far as Haines Junction, to say how many orders of trout they had for us, from the tourists on board. When they arrived half an hour later, they all thought the meals were wonderful and the service incredibly fast. Knowing in advance how many of the dinners we'd need, it was no trouble to time them almost to the minute.

8

Cooks!

Ned Mason and his wife Helen, a couple in their fifties, were sent to us by the Manpower office in Whitehorse. (Today, the employment centers are under the jurisdiction of the federal Employment and Immigration Canada department, which oversees the Canadian Unemployment Insurance program.) Ned was to be our bartender, Helen the cook. They arrived with glowing credentials and, with our initial optimism in our new venture, we welcomed them without a qualm; we were convinced that they were the answer to our needs right then. He would run the lounge like a pro, and she the kitchen. We thought.

Oh, the innocence and gullibility of the inexperienced.

Things seemed to be running smoothly enough for a few weeks, although it turned out that Ned wasn't in the best of health. Every afternoon he disappeared into their room, in the rear of the cafe building; we called it the cook's room. Helen always explained that Ned needed his nap in the afternoon, and that she could take over the bar and still attend to the kitchen chores. When the summer business picked up, though, I knew she would have enough to do, so I decided to spell him off myself.

It was then that I noticed our liquor stock was getting very low, even though we had just brought in a supply a few days ago. 'Something's wrong here,' I thought. 'It's time to take an inventory.'

While I was in the process of doing this, Ned showed up and offered to take over the job.

"I'm feeling fine now," he insisted.

As he reached across me for an ashtray, the smell of rye on his breath was overpowering. The truth hit me like a jackhammer. He had been drinking, every day. 'Wonder if he's PAID for any of it?'

"Oh it's okay Ned, I'd rather do it alone, thanks all the same," I replied.

The staff charge book was in the drawer of the cash register. My suspicions were justified when I found there were no entries for Ned. By the time I'd completed the inventory and checked all the till slips, there was no longer any doubt. Ned had managed not only to drink up all the profits but also to leave us with quite a deficit in the cocktail lounge department.

"Gordon," I said later, "they'll have to leave."

The thought of having to fire someone was distasteful—we'd never had to do it before. We decided to tell them that we would have to do without a bartender because the lounge wasn't paying off. Helen could stay on as cook but if Ned wanted to stay, he'd have to pay his own board. They stayed a few days longer but when he realized that I was always there when the lounge wasn't locked, charging him the same as anyone else for drinks, he decided they would try to find employment elsewhere.

This was also the beginning of a long procession of "would be" cooks, some of them lasting a month, others a few days. As I had no choice but to take on the job myself in the interim, we eventually decided not to fire any more cooks, no matter how incompetent, until we had another one hired and in the kitchen.

Shorty

One of the cooks was Shorty, also sent to us through the Manpower office. He was Chinese, and visions of chop suey and delicious deep fried prawns danced in my head when I heard he was coming. He is a wizard with steaks and western food as well, the girl in the office told us.

Impatiently, I waited for him to arrive and relieve me from the kitchen. When the day finally came, this little man got off the bus, walked up the steps of the cafe, and self-propelled himself into the kitchen. He was wearing a long and shaggy gopher-skin overcoat.

"You boss lady?" he asked me.

"I'm Mrs. Yardley, and this is boss man, Gordon," I told him. "This is your room, and after you put your things away, I'll show you where everything is kept. Then you'll be all ready to start in the morning."

"Yes—yes, I start in the morning."

I showed him around, and he disappeared into his room for the rest of the day.

'I hope he changes his shirt in the morning,' I thought. He was wearing a loud Hawaiian shirt that was a bit out of place in the kitchen, and none too clean.

The next morning, I awoke at six as usual. 'How heavenly,' I thought, 'we have a cook again—I can sleep in—it's been so long.' Wrong! In about half an hour—a knock on the door.

"Joyce, could you come over, please? We can't get the cook to take the orders. He just keeps saying, 'I wait for Boss Lady tell me what to do—you don't tell me!' "

Regretfully, I dragged myself over to the cafe. I finally convinced Shorty that it was okay, that he must take the food orders that the girls turned in.

So he began cooking—things that had no bearing at all on what had been ordered. I had to stand right over him saying, "No, no, Shorty, not eggs—pancakes!" In this fashion we got through the breakfast rush somehow, and I tried to calm the poor girls' frayed nerves by making a joke of his performance.

"We'll have steaks tonight," I told them. "The girl in Manpower told us he was a whiz with T-bones."

"Is he going to change his shirt?" Judy asked.

"I hope so," I said.

Shorty managed to make a pot of soup for the day, before retiring to his room. We were only hiring on one cook back then, so he had to be on a split shift; after the breakfast rush he would make the soup, then come back in the afternoon to prepare for dinner.

When Shorty emerged again, there was the unmistakable odor of liquor on his breath. He was all smiles, anxious to get to work. To test him out, I decided to have my steak early, before the crew arrived, just in case I would have to take over the grill myself.

"I'll have mine now, Shorty."

"Yes—yes, I cook good steak!"

And he busily went to work, making a great flourish of cooking it to perfection. I had to admit it wasn't bad at all. 'Maybe we can train him, yet,' I thought. Wrong again! Dinner was a disaster; we couldn't decide whether he was hard of hearing or whether he just refused to cooperate with the waitresses. One thing was very clear, though. He would have to go. Just as soon as we could get another cook.

Gordon's dad came to visit us the next day from Whitehorse. He walked into the kitchen and saw Shorty mashing a big pot of potatoes. Shorty was so short that he couldn't manage this on the counter. He had to put the pot on the floor, where he squatted down and mashed away with vigor. Pop whispered in my ear, "What rock did he crawl out from?"

Thank goodness the swinging door hid him from view of the customers in the dining room. I was doing the cooking again, and using Shorty for a helper. At least he could peel vegetables, mash potatoes, and do other simple jobs such as scrub the floors. We could keep him busy until we got someone else.

"Better get him to change his shirt," Pop said.

"We've tried," I told him with resignation. He would do anything else I asked him, but no one could persuade him to change that loud shirt.

When word came that a new cook was on the way, Gordon told Shorty that our regular cook was coming back; he had been sick but he was fine now.

"You be all ready in the morning; we need supplies in town, and you can catch a ride in with me."

"I stay here, I good cook."

"Sorry, Shorty, you and I are going into Whitehorse tomorrow."

The next morning, I came over early to begin the day's work, only to find Shorty there already. He had made the coffee and was preparing the pancake batter. He had changed his shirt!

"That's fine," I told him. "You have a nice breakfast. It's a long drive to town."

"No, Lady, it's for you—good pancakes," he said. "Shorty stay HERE."

'This isn't going to be easy,' I thought.

121

Gordon came in just then.

"You all ready, Shorty?"

"No, no, I stay with Boss Lady."

At that, I had to leave the kitchen. It was quite sad—but we had to do something. Gordon finally got him into the truck, and away they went.

Les

When the bus arrived an hour or so later, we met our next cook. Les was a dapper, wiry little Englishman. He made mouth-watering pastries, homemade bread, and rolls. His manner was always respectful. Personally, I found him a bit too deferential, but I was not complaining, believe me. It was such a relief to have finally found someone who could not only cook but also get along well with everyone. It looked like our troubles were over.

Wrong again! It wasn't long before we noticed certain bottles in the bar mysteriously missing. I just kept replacing them but, alerted now, I began marking the labels before closing the lounge at night, never saying a word about this to anyone. After a few weeks, the culprit became bolder—the liquor level was even lower from the marker in the mornings. 'Whoever is doing this must be filling another bottle, and taking it out,' I thought. After a while, though, there were whole bottles missing. We never really suspected Les, as he never frequented the bar in the evenings, or on his days off. Besides, we always locked the door between the lounge and kitchen at night before securing the entrance to the cafe.

One afternoon, Les made the mistake of coming on shift unmistakably tipsy.

"You'll have to talk to him, Gordon," I said.

"He'll just deny it. No, we'll have to catch him at it."

"But we've been trying for a month with no luck."

"I'll tell you what; tonight when we lock up, we'll stick around and see what happens."

That night, when the last customer left the lounge, I called to Gordon from the kitchen, knowing that Les could hear me as there was only a thin wall between there and the cook's room.

"Okay Gordon, I still have to clean the counter. Just lock the bar up and go on over if you want to—I can go out the cafe door. Be there in ten minutes."

Gordon locked both lounge doors but instead of going out, he stood just inside the entrance. I locked the cafe, slamming it as I went out, and went over to our room.

Gordon only had to wait a few minutes. Then, not ten inches from where he was standing, the front window began sliding slowly open, inch by inch. It was a Pierson window, with double panes, and somehow the latch had been opened on it during the day.

Les was standing outside, quietly pushing the window open with a long stick, a small flashlight in his shirt pocket. Gordon waited there in the dark until the window was open wide enough for Les to quickly slip in over the sill and start toward the bar.

"Got you, you sneaky little—" Gordon grabbed the little guy by the shirt collar and shook him until his teeth rattled. Then he opened the door and pointed down the road. "Now, get going—and KEEP going, if you know what's good for you!"

"I'm sorry, Gord," Les began.

"Never mind sorry, just get your butt out of here—NOW!"

With that, Les turned and started running down the road in the dark. Gordon came over and got into bed, still very angry.

"The little sneak! I'm sorry I gave him that 'advance' now. With the wages we pay him, he can certainly afford to pay for his booze."

"Well," I said, "I'm glad we caught him."

We both lay there, thinking our own thoughts, unable to sleep. I kept visualizing that little man walking down the road, shivering and alone in his thin white shirt.

"Did he have a jacket?" I asked.

"That's his problem," was the answer.

But I knew Gordon was worrying too. Suddenly, he could stand it no longer.

"Guess I'll have to take the pickup and go get him," he said gruffly. "He can go in the morning."

'Oh, thank goodness,' I thought.

An hour later Gordon was back.

"I couldn't find him," he said.

"Oh no! How far did you go?"

"A lot farther than he could have walked. I even stopped and checked the sides of the road."

"Someone must have picked him up before you went after him."

"Don't remember hearing any cars, do you?" Then a thought struck him. "I'll just have another look around the buildings here, in case he came back."

"Look in the bunkhouse," I said. "Maybe he's in there."

Ten minutes later, Gordon was back again, a grin on his face. He had gone into the bunkhouse—no one was using it this night, and it looked empty in the semidarkness. He was about to leave when a voice piped up: "It's just me, Gord, hope you don't mind."

"We'll go in to Whitehorse tomorrow morning," Gordon said, trying to keep the relief out of his voice.

The next day, they went into town and Gordon gave Les $100, which he didn't have coming, shook hands with Les, and wished him luck at the Manpower office, where he was heading to look for a new job.

One morning, our chambermaid took sick. We had been booked right up the previous night so there were a lot of beds to make and rooms to clean before we started renting them again. I cooked breakfast, made a huge pot of clam chowder, and left one of the waitresses to do the short-order cooking, as our new cook hadn't yet arrived, while I went over to the lodge to make up the rooms and do the laundry.

"Call me if someone comes into the lounge," I instructed as I left the girls.

Two hours later, I had the rooms cleaned and stripped. Then I carried in the sheets from the lines outside the old kitchen and piled them on the sofa in the lobby where I would fold them later to put through the mangle—this was the year before we put in the new laundry facilities. As I took in the last armful of the fresh, sun-dried sheets and threw them on the pile with the others, an irresistible urge to rest came over me. To go across the way and lay on our bed just seemed like too much effort, and that pile of sheets smelled so good, and looked so inviting, that I just slipped off my shoes and sank right into them, too tired to think of another thing.

It seemed like hours later when I became aware of a hand on my shoulder, shaking me gently, and a voice, seeming to come from a distance and slowly coming closer, urging me to get up.

"Go away and leave me alone—please let me sleep," I protested.

"The bus driver just phoned from the Junction, and Sally doesn't know how to cook fish," Judy said.

I ran into the bathroom, dashed some cold water on my face, and rushed back to the kitchen.

That night the lounge was full. We had found that the only possible way to make the lounge pay off was to run it ourselves. Gordon was on his way back from Whitehorse (I hoped with a new cook) but for now one of the waitresses, who was working a double shift, was helping me to serve drinks. We were both kept going full out until about two in the morning. When the reluctant customers finally left for the night, I went over to the lodge and fell into bed exhausted.

Gordon was already in bed, tired from the long day of picking up supplies and driving. I didn't wake him, figuring that if he had found a cook, he would have let me know.

At six o'clock the next morning, I got up with the intention of going over to the cafe to start breakfast, but found that my legs were just too weak to hold me up.

"Gordon, what will we do? I can't get breakfast; I'm too tired." I began to cry.

"I didn't tell you, but I brought a cook back last night. He was tired and just hit the sack in the bunkhouse when we got here. He said he'd look after breakfast, so don't worry about it. Just go back to sleep."

"But someone will have to show him the ropes first."

"Go back to sleep—they'll manage. I didn't get this one from Manpower. He's cooked for CNT and other government crews, and I just caught him between jobs. The fellows all know him and he's good."

With that, Gordon went over to the cafe and I lay there worrying, but too sick with what turned out to be a severe bout with the flu virus to get out of bed. Half an hour later, a knock came at the door and Judy came in with a tray. There was hot coffee, soft boiled eggs, and toast. There was even a rose on it—artificial, but I was still impressed. Judy was very excited.

"Don't worry about a thing. He's just taken over the kitchen like he's been there all his life, and everything's just perking. It's wonderful! We told him you weren't well and he fixed you this tray. Just rest up until you're feeling well."

'I must have died and gone to heaven,' I thought.

The arrival of Timmy, the new cook, was the turning point for us as far as our luck with cooks went. Never again would we go through Manpower when we needed one. We had learned our lesson. The rest of the summer went smoothly. We worked together as a team. With a competent staff and all of us cooperating, I began to relax again, and to enjoy the guests once more.

Timmy was excellent, and we were lucky enough to keep him for two summers. Then he was offered work, cooking for government road crews year-round, and we had to let him go as we could provide only seasonal work.

A friend of ours, Rita Olson, pitched in for a month or so, and we were treated to her delicious fried chicken, home-baked beans, and cornbread—no one could do it better. Her husband, Harold, whom we had known since 1943, had a fleet of trucks—some he owned himself, some were rentals—and a contract for hauling fuel from Haines to Whitehorse. He used the garage as a base for fueling the trucks, for tire repair, and general maintenance, and the drivers often stayed overnight in the bunkhouse. Of course, that meant they frequented the cafe.

Then there was Hazel Humme. Hazel had a large, grown-up family, which was scattered around the Yukon. Part Indian, she was a buxom woman with a big smile, warm personality, and big brown eyes that lit up her attractive face. Everyone loved Hazel. She was like a mother to us all, besides being an excellent cook— I can still close my eyes and taste her butter tarts and pies. She stayed with us for two years, then, tragically, her health broke down. We went to her funeral service, in the Anglican Church in Whitehorse. It was one of the saddest days in the lives of all her friends and family.

Randy

Randy was our next cook. He was working his way through University in Oklahoma City. He was an intern, with a couple of years to go before becoming a doctor. When we first met him, he was bookkeeper at a maintenance camp at Mile 94 on the Haines road.

Randy was young and ambitious, and looking for something more stimulating than keeping books. He turned out to be an excellent chef, with a flair for turning out mouth-watering meals—which he garnished so artfully that they looked as if they had come out of a magazine. We were beginning to gain a reputation for serving gourmet meals in the cafe.

Randy also organized and helped with the landscaping in front of the lodge. Just beyond the gas pumps was an unattractive section of ground which we now converted into a rock garden, planting trees and making a little pond with a Japanese-style bridge and a fountain. Randy figured out all the contours and levels, while the other men hauled trees, soil, and rocks, placing them where he suggested. The overall effect of the finished project was quite professional and added a great deal to the appearance of the buildings.

The next year, Randy arrived with his new wife, Shirley, who was a registered nurse, and she became one of our waitresses for the next two summers.

Gordon and I returned from Whitehorse one day from a shopping trip and found the cafe empty in the middle of the afternoon, except for Shirley, who was sitting there at the window with her knitting. This was most unusual for this time of the year.

"Where is everyone?" I asked her.

She looked slightly embarrassed as she replied, "Oh, they're all out in the back, behind the cafe. Randy shot a black bear this morning at the dump, and he's showing the staff and customers how to dissect it."

I couldn't believe my ears, but when we went out to investigate, sure enough, there was our chef with a bear carcass stretched out on a piece of clean plywood that he'd set up on a couple of empty fuel barrels. The little crowd around him was listening

127

raptly as he removed each organ, explained its function, and dropped it into a pail.

Oh well, I guess they were all furthering their education, and the tourists looked as though they thought it was great entertainment—not exactly what they had expected when they had dropped in for a meal but, after all, this was the Yukon.

Grandmothers Aren't Cute

To go back for a moment now, to the summer of 1961, our daughter, Norma, graduated from high school. Not long after that, she and Cal Waddington were married in Whitehorse. It seemed as though she had changed suddenly, from a bobbysoxer to a grown woman—while we weren't looking. As I watched our lovely daughter walking down the aisle on her father's arm, smiling at the young man we hardly knew—except for favorable reports from friends, and raves from Norma—I couldn't help but feel a sense of loss.

We had missed the last two years of her life in the hectic rush of our own. Looking at the happy glow on their faces, though, it was clear that something right was happening.

Cal was a radio announcer for CBC. A year later, we became grandparents, to a little boy they named Kurt. I was thirty-six years old when he was born.

When I got the news on the phone, I was the only one in the cafe. The others had all gone off shift, and Gordon and the boys were somewhere outside. I poured myself a glass of wine to celebrate, and sat there trying to decide what it felt like to be a grandmother. Something rebelled in me at the thought. *'I'm not ready yet. I don't feel OLD enough,'* I thought.

Gordon came in just then. "You're looking very serious and preoccupied."

I gave him the big news.

"Gosh," he said, "I'm not ready to sleep with a grandmother, yet." I immediately burst into tears. "That's okay" he teased, "You'll make a cute granny anyway."

"Grandmothers aren't CUTE!" I sobbed, and threw a menu at him.

By the time I woke up the next morning, my attitude had returned to normal, and with great excitement and anticipation, I waited to see our first grandchild. He would be another true Yukoner. Norma and Cal's daughter, Kris, came along a year later, and now their family was complete.

They volunteered to keep Ted, who was thirteen then, with them in Whitehorse so he could continue his schooling there. As Norma and Cal quite often came out to the lodge for the weekends, this turned out quite well. It was getting increasingly difficult trying to give the boys an education by correspondence at Dezadeash, what with so many diversions and interruptions. It seemed as if every time I'd go to check on them, I'd find Kirk out at the gas pumps and Ted out at the garage with one of the truckers, trying to talk him into letting him drive a huge Kenworth tanker from the garage to the fuel pump. Ted had started doing this when he was twelve. He was a small boy for his age, but with big ambitions. The truckers got a big kick out of teaching him how to drive their rigs. I would have liked to have given them a bigger kick for doing it, as he was supposed to be doing his school work.

One day a tourist, who had pulled up to the gas pumps, watched in his rearview mirror as a Kenworth truck started coming toward him. To his horror, he saw that it didn't have a driver. He stuck his head out the window of his car and yelled at Gordon, who was pumping gas into his car, "I'm getting this car out of here —there's a tanker heading in this direction without a driver!"

Gordon looked up and, sure enough, Ted was on his way, but being so small, from that distance and at ground level, all you could see of his head was just about two inches of hair.

"Well, something just changed gears in that truck," Gordon said. "I think you're safe enough."

I felt a little guilty about sending Ted to Whitehorse to stay with his sister at age thirteen.

Leon

Very seldom did we have a difficult customer. There was one fellow on the road crew, though, Leon, who seemed to carry a chip on his shoulder all the time. One morning when our cook was down with the flu, I came over to take the early shift. It was not one of my better days, as my throat was sore and I was very tired.

Leon was our first customer, arriving before the coffee had even perked. None of us quite had our bearings yet.

"How long does a guy have to wait for service around this joint?"

"It'll only be a minute, Leon. Can I get you some juice while you're waiting?"

"No! Don't drink the stuff—I want coffee right away."

"Coming right up."

"I want some decent sandwiches today, too. No more of that garbage you put in my lunch yesterday."

"Leon, I don't make the lunches, but you know perfectly well the girls are happy to put whatever you like best in your lunch. All you have to do is ask them."

"Yeah, sure! Blame it on the girls. I never get anything worth eating in mine!"

Our girls always made a special effort with the crew's sandwiches. Knowing the men had to take lunches every day, they would put a lot of time and thought into making them extra nice, tucking in little salads and deserts for variety. Leon just kept up the nagging.

Suddenly I had what can only be described as an "out of body" experience. Horrified, I stood back and watched myself go across the room to a small stack of lumber which the carpenters had left the day before, pick up a short piece of 2 x 4, and deliberately walk over to Leon, who sat watching me with a sneer as if to say, "Who does she think she's kidding?" Powerless to stop myself, I raised the board high above my head and, with wicked glee, saw his expression change to incredulous disbelief and fear—as I brought the board down with full force on his head. It felt so GOOD! I almost hit him again but I noticed a trickle of blood running down his forehead.

Sanity came flooding back; the devil departed from my shoulder. With a hateful look at the dumbfounded man, I turned and walked away, dusting off my hands. Once out of sight, I broke down and had a good cry. It all had a very therapeutic effect, and the rest of the day went very well.

The aftermath of the story was that I never heard another complaint from Leon. Ever. He even became quite friendly and treated me with great respect.

One of the staff members had witnessed the whole thing and the word quickly spread among the girls, who were ecstatic—he had given them all a bad time. The family had a hard time believing it at all, as it was so uncharacteristic of me to lose control that way. I had never hit anyone before, nor have I since, but Leon had pushed just a little too far.

9

Cortino Lodge

The Cortino family arrived on the scene in 1963, from Chicago. Jim had been to the Yukon several times before this on hunting expeditions; he decided he wanted to build or buy a lodge in the Dezadeash area. It would be an exclusive resort for hunters and fishermen, a getaway retreat for himself and his family; possibly an opportunity for his son and daughter—then in their early teens—to learn how to run a business in future years, away from the hectic and crime-filled life in Chicago.

Jim and his wife Buela had built and operated an old English pub back home called the "Come Back Inn Pub." It was a highly successful operation. They had fireplaces in each of the six dining rooms and three bars. His plans were to keep running it in the winter months and leave it with his brother in the summertime.

This time the family came up in a large motor home, mostly because their dog, Luke. A Great Dane pup the size of a small pony, Luke preferred this method of travel to being stuffed into his custom-made cage, which he was, frequently, for the family's flights to vacation spots overseas.

The first time Jim came to our lodge, he decided this was the one he wanted. He stopped by the cafe to see Gordon about it one afternoon. Gordon sent one of the girls over to get me.

"This is Jim Cortino—my wife, Joyce. Jim wants to talk to us about buying this business."

By this time in our career as innkeepers, I couldn't imagine parting with the lodge under any circumstances. It was just beginning to pay off, very attractively. We had reached this stage of development through much effort—sweat and tears—and life was finally becoming a little easier and more interesting all the time. I felt a pride of accomplishment in having survived all the hard knocks. And we'd made a lot of improvements. We still had many plans and projects yet to accomplish. We just couldn't abandon it all now.

Looking back, I realize that every major move we made evoked this kind of response in me. Pulling up roots has never been easy. Gordon always hates to have to tell someone "No," so I figured he was leaving it up to me to say it instead.

"I'm sorry, Mr. Cortino, it's not for sale," I said calmly.

"Wait a minute now, we can at least discuss it," Gordon protested, to my surprise.

"Maybe this will change your mind," said Jim, and lifted his hat up off the table to reveal a large roll of money. He had miscalculated. If he was seeking to impress, he'd come to the wrong person. Not trusting myself to speak, as I was not feeling very ladylike right then, I just turned and walked away, back over to the lodge. When Gordon came over, he was furious.

"You don't DO business that way!" he fumed. "You at least negotiate."

"But why lead him on if it's not for sale?"

"Anything's for sale if the price is right!"

It was anger speaking.

"Not in my books it's not."

The outcome of it all was that Gordon promised Jim that he'd think it over, apologized for my rudeness, and told him that he and his family could park in our yard and look things over for a few days.

Gordon eventually decided he didn't really want to sell yet. We never had to tell Jim, though. Having an Italian heart even bigger than his bank account, he came to us and said that he understood us not wanting to part with the business; he said that we would be good neighbors instead, as he would build a lodge just ten miles down the road, at the north end of the lake.

That is exactly what happened. Over the next five years, Jim and Beula built a luxurious H-shaped lodge from cedar logs, which blended nicely into the landscape. It had a relaxed and intimate atmosphere, featuring a cozy bar with a huge fireplace guarded by a stuffed albino moose, shot by Jim's friend and big game outfitter, Alex Van Bibber. And, on the shore of the lake, they built a beautiful log home and a dock with boats to rent.

Before long, they added ten horses and four Huskies to complete the picture.

The Cortinos hired a caretaker for the winter months, when they returned to Chicago to spell off Jim's brother in running their business there.

Klukshu Grizzly

Each fall we would say good-bye to our summer staff, as one by one they would leave to go home or, in some cases, back to school. The only ones left would usually be our faithful Mary, and Norman James, an Indian boy who helped us get our firewood every year. By November, the traffic, even from Haines Junction, would come practically to a standstill. Until the Haines Highway started being maintained in the winter months, we had to drain the waterlines, pack up anything that wouldn't stand freezing, and move to Whitehorse for the winter. We rented a house there, put Kirk into school, and brought Ted back home from Norma and Cal's house.

In the winter of 1963–64, we decided to keep the lodge open until Christmas, even though the business didn't warrant it. We wanted to find out what it was like there in winter.

An old Indian by the name of Jimmy Kane lived in a log cabin just past our big garage. As time went on, we got to know him very well, and we became good friends. Jimmy was an easygoing, philosophical type of man, who always had a smile. Nothing ever seemed to bother him. He had lived around Dezadeash, Klukshu, and Dalton Post all his life.

One day we were sitting by the window, at the staff table in the cafe, talking to Bun Beloud and a trucker friend who had come down from the Junction to see us. We were looking out across the lake when Jimmy Kane came walking by, on the way home from his trapline. I went to the door and called out to him.

"Hi Jimmy. Come on over and have coffee."

"I go light my fire first. I be there pretty quick."

It was early November and the temperature was twenty-five degrees below zero. Jimmy, who was in his eighties then, had his furs strapped on his back. Soon he was back, his teeth flashing in a big grin. His face was weathered and brown, a striking contrast to his white hair.

"Have a good day, Jimmy?" Gordon asked.

"Not too bad, not too bad. Save me from starving, anyways, until my check come." He turned to Bun. "Seen more bear tracks today—that BIG one," he said.

Because we were located only about sixty miles from the coast, as the crow flies, we discovered that Alaska brown bears would wend their way up the salmon streams and into our area. Some of them were quite a size. There was one elusive fellow in particular that seemed to frequent the streams and rivers in the vicinity quite often. His tracks were seen by several people—they measured 11 x 18 inches. He soon got to be known as Klukshu Grizzly, even though no one had seen him.

Grizzlies are not true hibernators. They will dig in under a bank or bunch of windfall, and are fairly dormant in the winter months. If their habitat is disturbed by glacier action that starts to seep in on them, however, or if a chinook comes along (that's a warm wind accompanied by higher temperatures, usually lasting for very short periods), the bears will be out on the move again.

A couple of big-game outfitters who worked the neighboring area, were offering their guides an extra $1,000, it was rumored, if they could locate the Klukshu Grizzly for their hunters. Jimmy Kane had come across his tracks in various places on his trapline, but had never caught a glimpse of the bear itself.

This was the animal Jimmy was referring to as he sipped his hot coffee in the cafe.

Bun, who was hauling fuel at that time from Haines, proceeded to tell us how, just the other day, he had driven around a sharp bend in the road and actually surprised the Klukshu Grizzly digging up gophers.

"I managed to get a shot at him as he was running away," Bun said. "The shell hit him, but he never even slowed down."

"If you shot him with that big rifle of yours, how the hell did he get away?" the trucker asked.

"Well," said Bun, with his typical brand of humor, "I wondered about that myself. I finally realized that in order to kill one that big, I'd have to shoot him on BOTH sides!"

We think it was that same bear that caused such a ruckus around our place later on that week. Old Jimmy Kane had gone in to the Junction to visit some friends. He had shot a moose only recently, and had left it hanging in the old shed he used for a meat cache. When he returned, he found that a bear had broken in and taken one of the hind quarters. A day or two later, he had to go to town again. Before he left, he asked Gordon if he'd keep watch on his place, in case the bear returned.

Unfortunately, that's just what happened; but he came when everyone was sleeping. When Gordon went over to check in the morning, he found that the bear had not only been back but also that he had broken into Jimmy's cabin. He had ignored the meat cache. It appeared that he had given the door a great whop with his paw and knocked it right off its hinges. He scattered cans of food and flour and jam all over the floor. Then, instead of going out the way he'd come in, he went out the window, which was too small for him; but he'd managed to get out anyway, breaking the glass and pulling all the casings off their nails in his struggle.

There was no sign of the bear that morning; only his tracks—huge black patches in the fresh snow leading around behind the lodge—were left outside.

Our son Kirk was sixteen years old at the time. He and Norman James used to go hunting together sometimes. This was fine with us, as Norman had been born and brought up in the bush. As well as helping with the firewood, Norman also helped to put up hay and, at times, took out fishing parties. Norman had never gone to school, but this fact certainly never tainted his opinion of himself. He had taught himself to read, mainly by learning what the labels on cans said. He had a sharp mind, a giant ego, and a good-natured friendliness about him. In later years, Gordon taught him how to run and operate his Cat. He seemed to have a natural leaning toward equipment and mechanics, and Gordon never had a better Cat skinner working for him.

Norman taught Kirk everything he needed to know about hunting and surviving in the wilderness, and the best way to handle a rifle. The two of them decided they wanted to go after this bear, who was becoming a nuisance, and also dangerous to have around where there were children a lot of the time. They had been using a 30-30, which apparently is too small for a grizzly. Knowing the risk involved, Gordon was reluctant to let them go, but the boys were determined; so Gordon insisted they at least take his new 30-06 as well. Off they went, tracking the bear into the woods.

All the signs pointed to a patch of willows about two acres in size that had heavy brush in the center and a few trees scattered through it.

"That bear's going to lie down," Norman said.

"How can you tell?" asked Kirk.

"If he wanted to go farther, he'd go around those bushes. This way, if he's going to sleep, he hears noise if something comes through brush. He wake up, and boy, you better be good shot or fast runner! This guy's BIG—pretty mad, too, maybe. You scared?"

"Not me! Why, are you?"

"Ho, you kidding—me? No bear big enough to scare me, kid."

"Let's go, then," said Kirk.

The boys made a big loop around the willows, just to make sure the bear hadn't gone right on through them; his tracks didn't reappear on the other side. They gingerly began picking their way through the middle of the thick willow. He was in here some-where—they knew this now. Farther and farther they crept, try-ing to peer through the bush, but not a sign or a sound greeted them other than an odd rabbit scampering out of the way as they advanced.

So suddenly it caught them completely by surprise, there was the Klukshu Grizzly right in front of them.

He spotted the boys at the same instant they saw him, and rose straight up from a sleeping position to his huge full height, standing on his hind legs and putting the boys in the position of looking way up at the bear. He was indeed a menacing sight, staring down like that, snorting and pawing the air, poised for battle.

In a split second, Norman swung the gun around and shot from his hip, as there was no time to take aim. The bear went down immediately, wounded badly. But with a roar of fury, he got up again. Next, Kirk let him have it with the 30-30, hitting him

137

just behind the ear. Thank God, this killed him outright. The boys had been lucky, though, besides being good marksmen, because many of these bears will get up and charge, even after being shot in the heart. This is a well-known fact, as bear hunters will testify.

When they measured him, stretched out from paw to paw, that bear was ten and a half feet wide, eleven feet long, and eighteen inches between the ears.

The boys also discovered that this old veteran had been in all kinds of trouble in his lifetime. The end of his nose had been split at one time and had healed, leaving a scar. His skull was lopsided, probably from some epic battle with another male bear in his younger days. They found numerous other scars as well; also that one eyetooth was broken off, while the other was worn down to half normal size.

Gordon asked Norman later, "Well, young fellow, what would you have done if you'd met that bear without having a gun along? Climb a tree or run?"

"What—me run?" he protested indignantly. "No way! I'd stand and fight like a man!"

Jimmy Kane repaired his cabin and the rest of his meat remained undisturbed.

It's All in the Way You Look at it

Kirk went to Australia when he was seventeen years old, exploring the interesting aspects of that country with a friend of his nicknamed Farmer. They worked their way around the island continent, trying out a variety of jobs, including sawmilling.

When Kirk decided it was time to come back to Canada, Farmer wasn't ready yet and tried to talk him into staying. He'd met an Australian Sheila that he liked. But Kirk came home anyway; his friend kept writing, telling him what he was missing. Farmer was an amateur poet of sorts but Kirk would never show me the verses he sent; he said they were too rough for a lady to read.

I was able to latch onto one, though. I found it to be humorous because he was obviously digging Kirk for not staying down under. It went something like this:

When bums get tired of bumming
And thieves get tired of theft;
When whores get tired of whoring
And there seems to be nothing left—

Then they congregate in gutters,
This low, belligerent scum,
And they flee like rats from a sinking ship
To the land of the Midnight Sun.

And they all end up in the Yukon,
Where the mountains meet the sky;
But they don't die off like an average plague,
NO—these bastards MULTIPLY!

It's all in the way you look at it, I suppose.

Kirk began his correspondence studies again, but the next winter, when we moved to Whitehorse, he decided to take a course in heavy duty mechanics and welding at the vocational school. He wanted to take over the garage at Dezadeash the next summer as a business of his own. Gordon was happy to turn it over to him and, young as he was, at eighteen years old, Kirk handled it very efficiently.

The Earthquake

Nineteen sixty-four was the year of the violent earthquake in southeastern Alaska. One hundred and fifteen people lost their lives in the disaster, most of them in the cities of Anchorage and Valdez. A tremor was all we felt at Dezadeash, from the quake itself, but the tragedy of the situation was brought home to us very vividly in the faces of the men and women who stopped by the lodge on their way south during the next few days. These were the families and individuals who were leaving the area forever. Some had lost their homes, others had lost friends or family members, and there were others who seemed to be still in a state of shock. They had to get away and try to put those awful memories behind them.

I remember one man, in particular, who came into the cafe one evening. He was carrying a load of expensive-looking camera equipment on his back, which he deposited on the floor in a corner. The man was probably around forty-five years old. He was wearing sunglasses, which was odd because the sun had gone down long before. He sat down at the counter beside two other people, a man and woman who were traveling in the opposite direction, to Fairbanks, Alaska, and struck up a conversation. As I poured his coffee, I couldn't help noticing how his hands shook as he lit up a cigarette. As I sat down at the staff table, I heard the woman ask him where his home was. He told her it was Anchorage.

"Oh, were you there when they had the earthquake?" she asked. "It must have been a frightening experience."

"Yes, I was there," he replied, "Oh, it could have been a lot worse. A lot of people couldn't take the suspense of the after-shocks. They didn't bother me, though."

Something in his voice didn't sound quite right to me, and I thought, 'Okay, lady, time to change the subject.' But the woman kept on quizzing him in detail about the disaster. Then, in the middle of a sentence, the man suddenly burst into tears. He got up, threw some change on the counter, and bolted out the door.

A shocked silence fell over everyone. Then Gordon noticed the man had forgotten to pick up his camera gear. He ran out with it and just caught the fellow as he was about to drive off. Gordon said the man's car was loaded to the roof with all kinds of household goods. It looked like he was one more of the folks who were clearing out for good. Our hearts went out to them all.

10

A Narrow Escape

In the winter of 1966–67, Gordon and I combined business and pleasure on a trip to Vancouver, late in December, to buy new linen, dishes, and other necessary replacements for the lodge. We stayed a few days with Gordon's mom and pop in Langley.

One evening we went to Murrayville to see an exceptional display of Christmas lights we had heard about. After enjoying the lights, we drove around for a while, then had dinner. Before heading for home, I said, "Let's go and have one more look at it." Gordon agreed.

We drove to the east end of Langley on the main road, then headed south to go across the Nicomekl River bridge. We were in the midst of a very cold snap and the bridge had black ice on it. Just as we were crossing (gingerly), I noticed a red glow in the water. I said, "That looks like a light down there, Gordon!" We stopped and got out of the car to check it out. Sure enough, we saw tail lights under the water. Then we hard a sound that made our blood run cold.

It was the faint sound of a baby crying, down there in the darkness of the river.

Gordon charged down the gully, shouting, "Run and get me some help."

I took off on the run across a field toward a farmhouse which I could see in the dim light. The field was still boggy and wet from recent rain, and I lost a shoe on the way. There was no time to slow down to retrieve it. I dashed through the doorway of the startled couple's house, almost out of breath, and gasped out the story to them.

The man of the house was gone almost before I'd finished the telling; his wife called an ambulance and the police, and I ran back to the car.

Gordon had struggled through the thick entanglement of blackberry bushes and thorns to find the car upside down in the water. He tried to get a door open but found the car had settled into the mud on the river bottom, making it impossible to pry the doors open. While he was wrestling with one of them, the farmer arrived to help. Between the two of them, they managed to get it open.

The mother shoved her two-year-old boy out through the opening, and Gordon brought him up to me in the car. The poor little fellow was soaked to the skin and shivering; but as soon as I wrapped him up in my coat, he stopped crying. He was wearing braces on his feet to correct a bone condition. The woman followed him out and, in a matter of minutes, the ambulance was there to take them to the hospital for observation.

We continued on home. When we got in the house, Gordon's mother noticed that his shoes were soaked. She began scolding, "I keep telling you to wear your rubbers in this weather." Then she stopped abruptly, round-eyed and shocked to discover he was soaked to the waist.

The next morning the lady and her husband came to the house to say thanks, and we heard her story. Apparently she'd been on her way home with the child when her car skidded on the ice, plunged into the river, and flipped upside down. It began slowly filling with water, which, when it had reached its level, came right up to the woman's neck. She had to hold the baby's head up to the floor boards to keep his nose and mouth out of the water.

At one point, she thought the back end of the car was higher than the front—and might have more air space. She ducked down under the water and into the back seat, only to find that there was even less air there; she had to go back into the front again, all the while holding the child's nose and mouth. With extreme presence of mind, she stayed calm while her mind raced in a desperate attempt to save her little boy's life. When she heard someone out there trying to get the door open, her relief must have been overwhelming.

Neither one of them suffered any ill effects from the episode, and it was a very grateful husband we met that day in Langley.

11

New Proprietors

If I could have looked ahead a few years at the time Jim Cortino was trying to buy our lodge, things may have taken a completely different turn. This business, we discovered, has a way of slowly wearing you down—to the point where you begin to think of giving it away lock, stock, and barrel to the next unfortunate customer who walks through the door. The novelty had worn off. We had accomplished what we had set out to do, and we were just plain TIRED.

"Maybe we should sell the place and turn our acreage into a ranch," I ventured, one day in 1967. I half expected an argument, or at least a curt, "You had the chance, five years ago." But this time Gordon agreed with me.

He had really been wanting to get that meadow in shape for a long time, but had never had time for clearing and rotovating; it was hard enough to find the time for haying in the fall. If a buyer comes along, we decided, we'll build a house—right where I'd always imagined one, in the middle of the meadow where Bun Beloud's haystack used to be. The prospect of just relaxing and cultivating the meadow to its full potential was so appealing that I could hardly wait.

It came as a big surprise when Norma and Cal decided they wanted to buy our business in the fall of 1967.

"Norma—no—you don't want it. You don't know what you're getting into."

"Yes we do. We've thought about it for a long time and we can handle it."

Despite our admonishments, they were determined. Norma is characteristically a determined person, and once her mind is made up, and provided she can convince Cal, there's no stopping her.

"We can always sell if it doesn't work out," she said. "Cal went to see the bank manager and he'll okay a loan for us. We're really ready for a change; we both want to get out of town for a few years."

Finally, we had to agree, and they became the proud new proprietors of Dezadeash Lodge, running it with all the enthusiasm that we had enjoyed in the early years.

Kirk still kept the garage end of the business, selling it to Norma and Cal at a later date.

Just one year after this, Cortino's lodge was finished—ten miles to the north of us at the end of the lake. The Cortinos' son Jamie was engaged, and their daughter Connie was flashing her big dark eyes at our son Ted, who was eighteen years old now.

"Aren't you spending an awful lot of time around Cortinos'?" I asked him.

"Well, Jim's new at the business, Mom, and he really needs someone with experience in that field."

"How about Norma and Cal? They're new at it, too."

He turned this over in his mind for a second or two, then came up with, "Yeah, but their waitresses aren't nearly as cute."

"You're not fooling me," I told him. "I've seen the way you and Connie look at each other."

But I knew he would do as he wanted, regardless of what I said.

Kathleen Lake Lodge

It was during this period that a young fair-haired girl from Norway turned up on the scene. Gunn Bakke had come north to work at the Haines Junction Inn for her uncle and aunt, John and Sally Bakke. She got along so well with Norma and Cal, however—not to mention Kirk—that she ended up helping out at Dezadeash instead.

On October 19, 1968, Kirk and Gunn were married in the little Anglican church at Haines Junction. We thought that he couldn't have made a better choice.

Then in the fall of 1969, Kirk sold the garage and service station to Cal and bought a property close to Kathleen Lake, between Dezadeash and the Junction. The property had a new

144

house on it, large enough for living quarters with enough space left over to convert into a cafe. They put in gas pumps and a service garage, and went into business, building rental cottages, installing showers for the public, and selling fishing tackle.

Kathleen Lake is not only one of the most scenic lakes in the Yukon but it also is famous for its good fishing, mostly landlocked salmon and lake trout. Kathleen River, which runs into it, is a good spot for rainbow trout. Needless to say, a large percentage of Kirk's and Gunn's business was from fishermen.

Before Kirk could put in a water system, he had to dig a well in the basement under the cafe. For this job, he approached Alex Taylor, a native of Dawson City. Alex agreed to do the job if they would provide a bed for him, as he didn't want to stay at the Junction.

"Those guys there drink too much," he proclaimed.

The job progressed very nicely, and Alex was down ten feet by Saturday night. As he was finishing his dinner in the cafe, a car pulled up to the gas pumps, and Alex went out to look after it. He came back in, handed Kirk the gas money, and said, "That's my friend, Shorty, out there. He's going to the Junction, and I guess I have to go look after him. Can I have some cash?"

"Sure," Kirk answered. "Guess we won't see you until tomorrow night then."

Alex knew it was important to get that well finished.

"No, my friend, you'll see me tonight. Don't forget, Alex keeps his word. You'll see."

With that, he went out and hopped into his friend's car. Well, Alex kept his word, all right. He even brought back a helper. About three o'clock in the morning, Kirk and Gunn woke up to the sounds of stumbling feet going down the basement stairs, and voices admonishing each other.

"Sh! Sh! Shut up, Shorty! Wanna wake up everybody?"

"You the one making too much damn noise, Alex. Why you blame me anyways?"

"You think I'm stupid—is that what you say, Shorty?"

"Oh, give me that bottle, and shut you face!"

After a bit, things seemed to quiet down for a while. Then, after what seemed like a long time, Gunn was awakened by a loud curse, followed by silence. She lay there, straining her ears, and soon heard a subdued, "Alex, where are you? Where ARE you Alex?"

No answer. Then, again and again, Shorty's voice saying, "Alex, Alex, where ARE you?"

"Kirk," said Gunn, shaking him gently by the shoulder.

"Something's wrong." Kirk pulled the blankets over his head.

"Something's WRONG, Kirk!" she repeated.

They both sat up and listened intently. As if from a great distance came a muffled cry, "Hulp, hulp."

"Alex, where the hell are you?"

The voice contained a hint of panic now.

"Hulp, hulp," the voice called again, only weaker now.

Kirk bolted out of bed, ran down the stairs, threw open the basement door, and found the light switch.

Sure enough, Alex had fallen down the well. It was a good thing there wasn't any water in it.

Freedom at Last!

Once we sold the lodge, it was like a burden had been lifted from my back. I felt almost euphoric—free-e-e, to do all sorts of things there hadn't been time for until then. The men had always taken the fishing parties out, so the first thing I wanted do was to go to Mush and Bates lakes.

I loved the peace and remoteness of those calm, clear, virgin lakes and their mirror-images of the trees and high, snow-capped mountains. The trail started out right behind our lodge; it led twelve miles to Mush Lake, which is about eight miles long and which is connected to Bates Lake, fifteen miles long, by a short river and waterfall. This took you right into the foothills of the St. Elias Mountains. I'm sure that only a very small number of people had fished there in the past. There were dozens of little bays with pebble beaches where we could pull up with the boat and have a picnic lunch, or just soak up the sun and wilderness sounds that were all around us. The ducks and loons were always making their presence known, and fish were jumping everywhere, sending out their ever-widening concentric circles in the water.

We could watch the beaver, at one spot, working away at their dams. They would cut a willow on a high bank above the trail and slide it down a chute they had dug or worn in the bank, drag it across the trail, and haul it into the water. One time we actually had to wait while they tugged away, not paying the slightest attention to us. They were far too busy.

There was a tiny cabin by the falls. The fishing there was excellent and we enjoyed many a mouth-watering meal of grayling. I would fry them in butter on the old wood stove, in the cast iron frying pan that no one ever removed from the cabin.

Very seldom did we make the trip without seeing a moose; sometimes we saw several of them on the same trip. There was a swampy area to one side of the trail that they particularly seemed to enjoy, and many times we would come across a big bull, with his head submerged, eating the tender shoots on the bottom. He would sense our presence as we passed and lifted an immense set of horns out of the water, turning to look at us. He didn't seem very worried, though, and soon went back to feeding.

This area is at its magnificent best in the winter. I used to ski up the trail toward Mush Lake, usually as far as Alder Creek and back, especially when the days would start to get longer and sunnier in the latter part of March or early April. At this time of the year, too, we often used our snowmobiles (or ski-doos, as we called them all, regardless of make).

The surface of the snow melts slightly during the day, then freezes hard again at night and forms a strong crust. Under these conditions, we could travel anywhere with speed and ease—over mountaintops and valleys—no trails needed then.

Every winter we'd go on at least one long trip. We would take as many friends as wanted to participate and set out for three or four days. We'd plan our route, load our toboggans with food, extra fuel, sleeping bags, either tents or tarpaulins, and whatever other supplies that were necessary—probably the most important item was matches.

We made one memorable trip in 1969, past Bates Lake and into the St. Elias Mountains, way back where there wasn't a living soul between the Pacific Ocean and ourselves. There were seven of us this time: Gordon and I; our friends Dorothy and Bob Vill from Haines; our son Ted; Joe Jacquot from Whitehorse; and Dave Hall, who was working at the lodge.

Everyone had his own machine, and we traveled over country that was way above timber line—the Wolverine Pass, it was called —and for twenty miles all we could see was snow-covered, undulating hills, the clear blue sky being the only color anywhere. There wasn't a tree in sight to break that pristine whiteness. Occasionally we'd go by some little bare twigs—the tips of alder bushes buried in many feet of snow. Around each of these were hundreds of ptarmigan tracks; a few times we scared up a flock of these birds as we approached. We could almost imagine ourselves being on the moon, especially when we came into country where the snow had built up into huge drifts and left craterlike holes in their wake.

After a few hours, we would take a break, bring out the thermos of hot coffee or chocolate, and have a snack. Then, in midafternoon when the sun was warmest, we could lie back on our machines and suntan, or have a snooze for half an hour. After a couple of days of this, our faces, at least, would be as brown as if we'd been to Hawaii.

When we dropped down out of Wolverine Pass, going toward Onion Lake and on to Silver Creek, we went down a thousand feet into a valley. There we hit a road that a miner had put in with his Cat a few years previously. The incline was so steep that he had to build it with many switchbacks, or sharp corners, to keep his pickup truck from picking up too much speed on the way down.

We took one snowmobile down this road at a time, one person riding and the rest holding the toboggans back with ropes in case the brakes gave out—in which case we could have plunged that portion of the thousand-foot bank that we still had to maneuver. Then we would hike back up and bring another one down.

A little way down the trail in the valley, we came across a lovely old log cabin. There was a huge set of moose horns over the door and lots of split firewood piled on the front porch. It was a sight for sore eyes. It meant that after a long and strenuous day—especially the grind down into the valley—we wouldn't have to pitch tents and make camp.

No one had likely used the cabin for many years, judging by the looks of it, but the wood stove was usable, and everyone was in high spirits as we had a hot rum and waited for the stew to warm up. After eating our meal, we spread out our foamies and sleeping bags, and in no time at all everyone was asleep.

Not for long, however. As the stove got hotter, the snow began to melt, and the roof began to leak—in various places. Some of us moved our beds over to the far side, making the others shove over—to the sounds of loud moans and protests over being crowded. This worked fine until the cabin got a bit warmer; then drip...drip.... Eventually, we maneuvered around until we were all between the drips and managed to get some sleep—even with Joe's snoring.

The next day we were on the trail again—having replaced the firewood in the hope that someone else would enjoy the lonely cabin one day—sailing over the crisp, clean snow in the sunshine and wishing it could go on forever. Our course had taken us in a large semicircle. We had started out on the trail going west to Mush Lake, behind the lodge, and would be ending up on the Haines Road, about thirty miles south of the lodge at Dalton Post, on the Tatsenshini River.

As we lost altitude, we found that the snow had started to deteriorate. To cross Silver Creek, the men had to fall trees and lay them across from bank to bank. There were a few places where they had to cut evergreen branches to throw over the soft spots on the trail so we could walk our machines over them, but, all in all, we made it back without any serious problems. Joe went back to Whitehorse, Bob and Dorothy to Haines, and our son Ted back to Cortino Lodge.

House on The Meadow

Ted came home one day in the spring of 1969 with the news that he and Connie were going to tie the knot in August. It didn't come as a surprise, but we felt that they were both far too young. I know Connie's mother felt the same way I did, but we had both been younger than these two when we had married their fathers, so we couldn't say too much.

Jim, however, was very enthusiastic about the coming wedding, and proudly introduced Ted to everyone who came by as his future son-in-law.

"They're going to run this place," he said. "I'm going to turn the whole place over to them."

They had a beautiful wedding at Cortino Lodge, on August 29, 1969; Norma and Gunn were among the bridesmaids, and Kirk and Connie's brother Jamie stood up for Ted. Jim cried harder than anyone else. We had a wonderful Italian feast afterward.

In the meantime, we had built a temporary but comfortable little cabin on the meadow and started work in earnest on the new home. We put in four big picture windows, three in the living room and one in the bedroom, each one framing a view of the high mountains all around us, with the meadow in the foreground.

We built a fireplace, with stonework spanning the wall from the floor to the ceiling, out of hand-picked rocks. We traveled for miles collecting the rocks, even going across the Tatsenshini River with our jeep to gather some pinkish-hued ones on a creek bottom. My brother-in-law had a lot of experience with fireplaces, so we put him to work.

Our long driveway cut through the field to the road, where we built a gateway with a huge yellow arch made out of eight-inch pipe, and a sign that said Hay Meadow.

We purchased new haying equipment and built a large shed to keep it in, as well as a hay barn. Gordon put up the hay himself for the first couple of summers; when they had time, Norma and Cal, and sometimes Kirk, came down and helped. After that, we entered into a joint venture with a friend from Haines Junction, Rod Tait, to cut and bale the hay; Rod received a percentage of the yield, and we supplied the equipment. A few years earlier, Rod had been superintendent of an experimental farm that the government owned three miles north of the Junction. It had been shut down, after twenty years. Rod had bought the cattle from the farm and kept them on his meadow at the Junction; he needed all the hay he could get to feed them. It was a good arrangement for both of us and we soon found that Rod was a hard-working and highly motivated man.

Gordon cleared and rotivated the undeveloped areas with his D-7 Cat, while Rod did the haying. It wasn't long before we were producing 6,000 bales a season. Rod also fenced in the meadow to keep out the stray horses that roamed in the vicinity. Keeping out the moose in the fall, however, was a different matter. Their thick hides seemed impervious to the barbed wire, and Rod was forever having to repair spots where they had crashed through the fence. I remembered Bun having told us about continuously having to drive them away from his haystack.

I loved watching the wild animals that were frequent visitors on our meadow. We saw coyotes, wolves, and foxes, an occasional bear, and many rabbits. The meadow was also a haven for migrating birds. The north side of the meadow borders the lake, and tall grass used to grow thick along the shallow shoreline. In May, the place would be alive with snipe, mallard ducks, snow geese, and, once in a while, we'd see a swan or two.

Our dinner table was at the north window. There was a swale, or depression in the ground, just outside which became a small pond when the snow melted in the spring. We would have our meals and watch the mallards with their bright green heads swimming around and feeding on the tender shoots under the water.

Canada geese would visit us twice a year on their journeys north and south. And just in case life became too pleasant, the swallows would arrive in droves each year to stucco our house and garage, refusing to be discouraged by all the plastic ribbons and eagle decoys that we tacked up on the eaves. Gordon even built a special swallow house for them, on a long beam which he hung with chains on the back wall of the garage; but they preferred the view from the front, I guess.

Then there were the mosquitoes and black flies. These lasted only a few weeks, though, and we could cope with them by using mosquito spray.

Gordon had put in a pipeline for water, from a creek nearby. This was only functional in the summer, unfortunately, so we decided to put in a well—by driving a gravel point into the ground. The men decided the best place for it would be right under the house, so it wouldn't freeze in the winter. They rolled up the carpet; removed some boards from the floor in the living room, and began driving in the steel pipes. It was so noisy that I decided to get out and pick some black currants, which grew in profusion all along the edges of the meadow, where the ground had been disturbed by the rototiller.

When I returned with my berries, I noticed an unfamiliar car in the driveway. It turned out to be John Schmidt. We hadn't seen John since our Carcross days. John, an editor with the *Calgary Herald,* was watching, fascinated, while Gordon and Kirk drilled for water in the middle of our living room. I couldn't figure out why he considered this so odd. Stranger things happened around our place every day.

John was evidently impressed with our meadow, as we received a *Herald* article by him later in the mail; it was entitled "Canada's Most Beautiful Ranch."

The well project, sadly, was not a success. Sufficient to say, we continued to haul our water in the winter months for the balance of our years on the meadow. In spite of all this, we spent some of our best Christmases there, and Easters as well. The family would come down with the grandchildren and we'd all go skiing or snowmobiling for most of the day. Then we'd come in, shed our wet mitts and moccasins, hang up our snow-caked clothes to dry behind the wood heater, and pitch into a hearty dinner of turkey, which had been put in the oven early to cook—which it did to golden perfection—while we romped in the snow. They don't make turkeys the way they used to—or maybe our appetites don't get the same chance to become whetted as they did in those days. I think we've all become couch potatoes.

Well, a couple of us, anyway.

12

Prospecting for Copper

Old Jimmy Kane enjoyed talking about the old days. He also had quite a hankering to go prospecting, and would try to persuade Gordon to go out and investigate some mineral showing he always thought "look pretty good to me!"

There was quite a bit of prospecting going on in the Tatsenshini valley around this time, particularly for copper, which was in high demand. Jimmy was aware of this. One day when he dropped by for coffee, he said to Gordon, "I know where there's copper not far from here—cross the Tatsenshini. I see it long time ago. Maybe you better stake him."

Gordon knew of this spot, too. He said, "I've thought of that from time to time, Jimmy. Just haven't had the time to do anything about it."

"Why don't you make time, and go with him?" I asked. "It doesn't take that long to stake a few claims."

"Well, tell you what. You and Jimmy go and stake it, and I'll sell it for you."

Gordon was half kidding, but my interest was piqued by that time.

It was early spring, with some snow left in the bush. I couldn't give up the idea, and finally Gordon agreed to take us out to stake the ground.

We set out in the pickup, and by the time we had tramped around, cutting the stakes, pacing the distances, and putting the stakes in the ground, it was getting dark. We found a big tree for shelter and Gordon and I rolled out our sleeping bags where the ground was dry, under the spreading branches. Jimmy just had a blanket, and he rolled up in it under another tree. I wondered if he'd be warm enough, but he knew what he was doing; he slept like a log.

The stars were bright and twinkling, and the air was crisp and cold, but inside the bag it was toasty warm. I watched the stars as long as I could before my eyes closed in spite of myself, and I fell asleep. Surprisingly, the sky clouded up during the night, and when we woke up in the morning, there was a light layer of snow over the lower half of our sleeping bags, the top half being still in the shelter of the tree. We shook out our bedding, rolled it up, made a campfire, and had breakfast. There was another stake or two to finish up, then we drove home.

Not long after that, a fellow we knew by the name of Johnny Amato showed up at the lodge and booked a room. Gordon ran into him in the cafe.

Johnny said, "Do you happen to know of any copper showings around this part of the country?"

"Why yeah, as a matter of fact, I do," said Gordon. "I staked some just last week."

Johnny was a promoter, always looking for a deal on mining property.

"What do you want for them?" he asked.

"Oh, I don't know," Gordon replied. "Haven't given it much thought."

"I think I'll form a company on the property," said Johnny. "I can pay you all in shares—or part shares, part cash—you name it."

"Well, to tell you the truth, I'm not much interested in shares, but I'll give you a good deal on this one. How about $5,000 cash?"

"You've got it, man!" said Johnny, and wrote out a check right there.

The next time we went to Whitehorse, we took the check into the bank, half expecting it to bounce. To our surprise, it was a good one. We put half of it in our account, and took $2,500 back to Jimmy Kane.

We found out later that Johnny, the promoter, had turned around the next day and sold the property for $35,000 to a mining man in Whitehorse, who, in turn, added more claims to it and formed a mining company called Jackpot Copper. For the next several years, the company prospected and drilled the ground, but the drilling results didn't prove up well enough to continue the operation and it shut down.

"Gosh, I dunno about this stuff," said Jimmy, when we gave him his share of the money. "Maybe you better keep it for me, and I get a little bit at a time—when I need it, you know?"

So we became Jimmy Kane's bankers.

Once a month, Jimmy used to get his government check in the mail, and he was off to the Junction. There he had lots of friends, just waiting to help him spend his money in the beer parlor.

If he had any left to buy a few groceries after that, he was lucky. I guess Jimmy was afraid his $2,500 would slip out of his hands the same way. Periodically, after that, he would come down to our house on the meadow and get some money from us, usually $100 at a time.

One day we were eating our lunch and looking out our picture window when we saw a pickup approaching down the driveway. It was Jimmy, and his son was driving. They pulled up outside the house, where Harvey stayed while Jimmy came in.

"How are you making out these days?" asked Gordon, as I poured Jimmy a cup of tea.

Jimmy's round face was beaming. "Good, good," he nodded. "You see that truck out there? That belong to my son. And see the boat on back? That his too—and a fifteen-horsepower motor."

"That's pretty good, Jimmy," said Gordon. "Did Harvey get a job somewhere?"

The old fellow looked at him as if he had holes in his head.

"Who, Harvey?" he asked incredulously. "You know Harvey don't work; but his wife—she work all time though. Yes, my boy Harvey, he think pretty good now. Only son I got, you know," he proclaimed proudly. "We gonna go Junction now."

"Guess you'll need some money, then."

"Oh, not much—maybe $1,000," he answered.

Visions of Jimmy's money going down the drain very quickly ran around in Gordon's mind.

"You're sure you want that much, all at one shot, Jim?"

"Yes, I gotta pay bills and buy groceries."

"Okay, here you go—you take care of yourself, now."

We watched the pickup going back down our long driveway and out to the highway.

155

It was about ten days before we saw Jimmy again. Gordon was up at the lodge fixing a tire in the yard when one of the tanker trucks that hauled fuel from Haines every day pulled up, and out climbed Jimmy. He saw Gordon working on the tire and came over. He looked pretty saggy, walking across the yard; all his usual bounce was gone. He had one whopper of a hangover.

"Well, hi there, Jimmy, how's the world treating you?"

"Not very good, Gordon," said Jimmy. "I tell ya, boy, it's sure pretty tough to be rich."

We Become Trappers

"You still young fella," Jimmy said to Gordon one day. "You should take over that trapline now. I want you to trap it; I'm old man now—my legs not too good now; I show you how to trap." 'If his legs are no good now,' I thought, 'and he still hikes twenty miles or more on his trapline, I wonder how many miles he walked when he was young?'

"What about your son, Jimmy? Maybe he wants your trapline," Gordon said.

"Oh he lazy, too, sometime. You know young people! You gotta run it you own self."

Traplines in that part of the country were in designated areas and could be trapped only by the registered trappers. Jimmy's trapline was fifteen miles wide and fifteen miles long. It was bordered on the west by the Haines Highway, stretched to the British Columbia border, and took in Klukshu and Howard lakes, which lay at the head of the Takhani River.

In 1971, we bought the trapline from Jimmy. There was a sideroad about six miles long just south of the meadow. We took the pickup that far and unloaded our snowmobiles. Then we had to decide just where we wanted to make the trail we'd be using for the rest of the winter to run our traps. It would have to be wide enough for our snowmobiles, but too narrow for jeeps and four-wheel drives to use; we didn't want anyone scaring the animals away. We snowshoed over the route first, carrying an ax and power saw to blaze the trees and cut through windfall. The next day, we took our machines up to where we had left off working.

At nightfall, we headed back home to our house on the meadow, and went at it again the next morning. After a few days of this, we had a well-packed trail reaching seven miles into the wilderness.

The next job was building our trapline cabin. For this, we cut the logs right on the site. Gordon cut them on a slope, limbed them, and showed me how to take them over to where we were building. I'd place a short portion of a tree under one end of the log, to use as a roller, then pick up the opposite end and push it along the roller until it was about halfway; then I'd slide another roller under the far end of the log and push some more. In this fashion it was fairly easy to roll the logs right to where we needed them.

We took in a load of supplies, nails, windows, and the like on a couple of packhorses, and before long we had a very comfortable little cabin, with two bunk beds, a barrel heater, a washstand, a table and chairs, a radio, and propane lights. I chinked the cracks between the logs with moss—there was lots of it among the trees, the nice, deep sphagnum type. This moss is bone dry in the north during the cold winter months, as there is little or no humidity then. It kept the cabin toasty warm. We put in a double door in case we had to take our snowmobiles inside to work on them in extremely cold weather. Many times we were thankful we had thought of that possibility.

Having a trapline, I discovered, meant continually breaking trail with our snowmobiles. Sometimes after a heavy snowfall, we had to depend on the blaze marks we had made on the trees to even find our trail. The well-packed base was still there, but no longer visible; we had to pack it down once more. It was important to stay on that old trail because if you slipped off, your machine could get mired down in deep snow. When the weather is freezing cold, the snow has the consistency of dry sugar, with no packability. It is almost impossible to get the necessary traction to get out of a deep spot. It would take both Gordon and I to get the heavy machines back on the trail when we did slip off it, Gordon half pushing, half lifting it, and me working the throttle while walking alongside in snow up to my waist.

I soon learned not to get behind on the trail, after trying to get my machine out of a hole by myself a few times. Gordon was not very far ahead of me on those occasions when I got stuck, but although I shouted at the top of my voice, he never heard a thing above the loud noise of the motor. He eventually turned around and discovered that I was out of sight. To turn a heavy snowmobile around on a narrow trail when conditions are like that is a lot of work. He had to tramp, or sometimes shovel, a turnaround in the snow, come back to help me out of the hole, and then make another turnaround to get facing in the right direction again. Needless to say, I wasn't very popular when this happened; it either invoked a stony silence and disapproving looks on Gordon's part, if he figured I had been careless, or a lively shouting match, if I was convinced that the accident was unavoidable. As I said, I soon became quite skillful in maneuvering that snowmobile, and in keeping up. When Gordon slipped off the trail—he did, now and then—I tried not to look too triumphant.

One time when we were crossing Klukshu Lake to run our traps along the shoreline, a storm came up suddenly and we found ourselves facing a blizzard. The wind whipped the snow up from the ice and drove it into our faces; it felt like sharp ice crystals being driven into the flesh. I wrapped my long woolen scarf around my face and soon it was caked with snow, with little icicles forming from my warm breath. Visibility was just about nil, but we managed to get to the shore and into the shelter of some trees.

I always wore a one-piece nylon snowmobile suit with an eiderdown lining and heavy zipper; the hood had wolverine fur around the face. This, plus nylon boots with felt liners and moosehide mitts on a long cord which went around my neck, kept me toasty warm as long as we were moving. Gordon liked the freedom of his two-piece outfit—down jacket and heavy woolen pants.

When the wind began to subside, we broke some dry twigs from the trunk of a large spruce tree and got a small fire started. We brushed the snow from some stumps and sat there warming our hands and drinking hot coffee from the thermos.

"You can stay here, if you like, while I go over and run the traps around the next point," Gordon offered. "Then we'll head for home."

By then, the storm was over and the sky had some blue patches in it, but I decided to wait. As Gordon disappeared around the point, with the small toboggan in tow, I wandered out on the ice to keep my circulation up. Even bundled up as I was, a person could get cold if she just sat still when it was minus ten degrees Fahrenheit or lower. The trail left by our snowmobile tracks was smooth to walk on, and I must have been half a mile from shore when the sky clouded over and the gusty winds started blowing again. I was caught in an unexpected gale, with no snow-mobile to hang onto. I turned my back to the wind to catch my breath for a few minutes. The wind was whipping the snow by me at lightning speed. Suddenly, as I watched it, I was gripped by an overpowering sensation of being hurled backward on the ice. The snow had stopped moving, it seemed, and now it was me speeding backward on my feet over the ice—driven back with such force that I became dizzy, losing my breath and then my balance, clutching at empty air to keep from falling. Panic-stricken, I closed my eyes; immediately the feeling was gone. Thank heavens! It had only lasted a few seconds but it was very frightening. As an experiment, I turned to face the driving wind and snow and, sure enough, the sensation returned—only this time I was hurtling ahead instead of backward. But now I knew just what to do, and I closed my eyes for a moment.

The fury of the wind died down as suddenly as it had come up, but the walk back to my snowmobile was not as easy as it had been a bit earlier. Small drifts had formed across the trail already. I trudged through them, thinking about that fast-moving snow and how it had affected my equilibrium out there on the ice. I thought about the title of a poem I had read once, "Who Has Seen the Wind?" I was glad that the wind was invisible most of the time.

Gordon pulled up at about the same time I as reached the shore. He had a wolverine carcass and two lynx on the toboggan.

Something we had to always be on the watch for on the lake was slushing conditions. As the snow gets heavier on the ice, water is forced up in places; sometimes it can be several inches deep, on top of the ice but still under the snow. If we had to cross a spot that looked suspicious, Gordon would go first with his machine to check it out, sometimes getting off and walking ahead a bit, thrusting his ax handle down into the snow at intervals. I would follow behind at a respectable distance—no sense getting two machines bogged down.

Sometimes, though, it would be unavoidable, and we'd get into places where we couldn't see that the weight of the snow had caused slush to form—until it was too late; then it would take an awful lot of effort to push the machines out of there. Somehow, though, we always managed to get them out and back to the cabin before the water and ice froze up the tracks. This was the very reason we had put a double door on the cabin, and we'd drag the machines inside.

Gordon used to do the skinning when we went back to our house on the meadow, as there was a good garage there with more room to hang the stretchers for drying the furs.

We enjoyed the quietness of the trapline, and the clear, cold walks in the evenings when the only sound would be the crunching of our moccasins on the snow, which sparkled like diamonds in the moonlight. Occasionally we'd hear some coyotes yapping in the distance, or a couple of owls hooting back and forth to each other, but we were many miles from other human beings—and the sounds of car motors.

'If only we didn't have to kill the animals,' I thought privately.

There was a pack of about thirteen wolves that circled our cabin every three weeks. By observing them closely over the winter, and conversing with some Indians, we found out they traveled in a radius of about a hundred miles. Some nights we could hear them howling down the valley about eight miles or so away. The next night they'd be right around our cabin. And the next night, they'd be four or five miles beyond us.

Wolf packs are very close-knit families. If one gets too old to fend for itself, the pack will kill a moose, leave it for the old-timer, then travel on; they have to be on the move all the time to find enough food for the pack. One night they dropped an old one off close to our camp. Night after night after this we'd hear his solitary howl. He sounded so lonely that Gordon used to go outside and try to imitate his sound to keep him company. Each "ow-oo-oo-oo" would get a reply from the animal—and the two

160

of them would howl back and forth across the little lake in the frosty moonlight. When Gordon got tired and gave up, the old wolf would whine and yelp, almost as if he was disappointed that the game was over.

We never tried to trap the wolves. It just didn't seem right. For the lynx and wolverine which were so plentiful on our trail, we used the Conibear traps to ensure the animals would be killed instantly, without suffering.

The Second Year

A young friend of ours, Mike Crawshay, gave us a hand with the trapping during our second winter on the line, as he wanted to learn the business. He had worked during the hunting season with a big-game guide from Haines Junction. Mike was the perfect companion for us that winter; he loved the outdoor life, was eager to learn, and his help and energy was certainly appreciated by us both. For me, it meant not having to run the traps every day with Gordon, but only when I felt like it. I even had time to read books and bake pies now.

Mike decided it would be a good idea to put out a few snares to catch a rabbit or two for dinner. I had no idea where he had set these traps, or if indeed he had carried out the plan at all—until several days later.

Once or twice in midwinter, a warm spell with chinook winds from the south would come along. It usually lasted only one or two days, and it felt pleasant and balmy during that time. The consistency of the snow changed noticeably, even in that short time, and became easier to pack—snowman weather, I used to call it. On one of these warm, sunny afternoons while the men were visiting over a cup of coffee, I went for a long walk on a narrow foot trail that turned out to be Mike's rabbit snare line. I was on my way back to the cabin, breathing in the fresh, clean air and enjoying the welcome sunshine, when I was stopped dead in my tracks by the sound of a baby crying. 'It can only be a rabbit,' I thought. I had heard that they made a sound like this when they are hurt. Sure enough, I came onto the poor little thing caught in a snare, but trapped around the middle instead of its neck, which is where snares are supposed to catch them. Knowing that I couldn't free the animal myself, I set off on a dead run for the cabin. I burst in, out of breath and in tears, and yelled at the startled men, who were still sitting at the table.

"One of you go and either let that rabbit go or put it out of its misery, right now!" They looked at each other in disbelief. "Right this minute, do you hear? Or I'll never cook another meal for you as long as I live!"

Mike was out of the cabin like a shot while Gordon tried to get me calmed down. It took a little while.

Gordon and Mike thought they should build a shed next to the cabin for skinning the animals instead of taking them to the meadow house. It didn't take long to improvise one out of the left-over plywood we had piled under a canvas in the yard. The next night, after running the trapline and having dinner, the men went out and started skinning a couple of lynx in the shed, by the light of a lantern. I went to bed with a book. An hour or so later, Gordon came inside, washed up, and decided to turn in, too.

"It's getting pretty cold out there," he remarked.

"I can tell that by your feet," I answered as I moved closer to the wall. In the middle of the night, I woke up itching all over. 'What in the world's going on here?' I asked myself. Try as I might, I couldn't get back to sleep. When daylight came, I discovered little welts all over my body. An awful suspicion began to dawn in my head.

"Gordon, do those lynx have fleas? Just look at this."

He looked a bit guilty, but I wasn't getting any sympathy from him. "I don't have any bites, but then, why should they stay on me when you were so nice and warm last night?" I never seriously considered leaving Gordon—just killing him.

It turned out that Mike wasn't bothered by the insects, either. I was the only one. And after the same thing had happened a few more times, I reluctantly decided I'd have to stay behind in the house on the meadow for the rest of the winter, because I was definitely allergic to the fleas those animals carried. I was glad that Gordon had Mike to help him with the trapping.

The next winter, Gordon put the trapline on hold and went into live trapping instead. It had become harder and harder to kill the animals. I guess neither of us were cut out for it. We had both arrived at the point where we would be hoping the traps would be empty when we ran them.

There was quite a demand for wolverine at the game farm in Whitehorse right then, so Gordon made some cages to catch them. He welded together a couple of twelve-gallon aviation fuel drums to make a long barrel fifteen inches in diameter. Then he welded heavy crusher screen over one end. He made a "drop-door" out of the same screen and put it inside a framework, which he then welded onto the other end of the barrel. This sliding door was triggered to drop down and lock when an animal entered the barrel.

Gordon used partly decomposed ducks for bait. Wolverine are extremely wily animals and will not normally be hoodwinked into going into anything unfamiliar to them. They also have a cranky disposition, and a bad, bad temper.

Gordon used to throw one duck inside the barrel and hang another one in a tree beside it—just high enough that a wolverine couldn't quite reach it.

When one finally came along, attracted to the odor of the rotting ducks, he'd sniff at the one in the barrel, but never have enough nerve to go in after it. Then he'd notice the one in the tree. After trying over and over to reach it, he would get so mad and frustrated that he would dive inside the barrel, grab that dead duck, and devour it in one gulp—only to discover that the heavy door had clanged shut behind him and he was a dead duck himself. Or could have been.

Luckily for him, however, it was not his hide we were after.

Gordon always threw an armful of dry straw inside the cage, because when a wolverine discovers that he is trapped, he will fight to get out until he's wringing wet. He snarls and roars and shakes the bars on the trap door until he's exhausted. Then he'll roll over and over in the straw, which helps to dry him off and keeps him from getting pneumonia.

Once Gordon had one of these animals in the cage, he'd lose no time sliding the trap into the pickup and running it in to the game farm in Whitehorse, where Danny Nolan would be waiting for him.

163

The wolverine would be transferred to a large and comfortable enclosure, and fed. Incidentally, it was Danny who had taught Gordon the duck trick.

13

The Fire

In 1971, Norma and Cal decided they'd had enough of the lodge business. They had been successful at running the lodge, but Cal felt it was time for a change, after three years. He decided to try freelancing for a while, making documentaries and working as a photographer. They put the business up for sale and purchased some property, not far from the lodge, where they could build a home. Like us, they weren't ready to leave that part of the country yet, and their children, Kurt and Kris, were still going to school at the Junction.

They didn't have to wait long. A couple by the name of Heintz and Katie Eckervogt from Germany came through one day, liked the look of the lodge, and, noticing that it was for sale, found Cal and started asking questions. Before the day was over, they had made up their minds to buy the business. Soon after that, they went on to Whitehorse, where they caught a plane back to Germany to get their business affairs in order.

"I'll send my partner up to sign the necessary papers," Heintz told Cal.

About a week later, Heintz's partner, Delbert Lein, arrived. He had, indeed, come to finalize the sale of the lodge. He booked into a room, then proceeded to celebrate the acquisition of the lodge in the lounge. Delbert, nicknamed Superstar, must have been about eight feet tall. He was a thin, angular man who seemed to be all arms and legs, a likable character who soon made a hit with the whole staff.

Tomorrow they'd get down to business and sign the deal, he said. An hour or two, and many drinks, later, he took off (rather unsteadily) for his room.

Down on the meadow, across the road and less than a quarter mile south of the lodge, Gordon and I were preparing for bed. I opened the door to let the dog out, glanced up, and saw the flames shooting up into the darkness.

Fear stabbed me in the stomach like a knife. Gordon said my face was dead white when I ran in and choked out, "The lodge is on fire!" The rest of the night was like a nightmare. We jumped into the pickup and raced to the lodge. It was already an inferno. Cal and some men who happened to be around that night were up on the roof of the lounge, trying to keep the flying sparks and burning embers from setting fire to the other buildings. They were batting out the sparks with their jackets and reaching for the buckets of water that the waitresses were passing up the ladder to them. The girls filled the buckets at the sink in the cafe.

Our only water source there was a nearby creek, from which we had a pipeline and gravity feed to the buildings. There wasn't enough water pressure, though, for a hose on a job like that. Some of the staff were piling all the chairs and shelf stock from the cafe outside on the ground.

The fire department from the Junction came down but, by the time they got there, it was too late for the lodge, and the other buildings were already out of danger. A good friend, Chuck Egli, Cal, the waitresses, and the customers who stayed to help had saved the bunkhouse, the girls' cabin, and the cafe. The next morning, the cafe, at least, was open for business as usual.

Chuck had jumped onto a D-7 Cat that a pipeline construction outfit had left parked by the garage, wrapped a wet blanket around himself, and delved right in—pushing back the burning debris to keep the fire from spreading. When he came in the cafe later, his face and hair were black from smoke and soot.

When the fire was first discovered, Cal had rousted everyone from their rooms—except Delbert, who was sleeping so soundly they had to break the door to get him out. He was pretty shaken up, but physically okay.

Jim Cortino had seen the fiery glow on the skyline and driven over from his lodge ten miles away. He very kindly offered free rooms to everybody who needed them for the rest of the night, including our staff.

Crestfallen and sizing up the damage—the lodge was just a rubble of burning coals, which the insurance couldn't begin to cover—Cal figured for sure that the sale would be off now. Surprisingly, though, after making some phone calls to Heintz, Delbert said they still wanted the business. They estimated the cost of building a new lodge, made some adjustments in price, and the deal went through.

Norma and Cal built an attractive lock-stave cedar home on their property, which adjoined our meadow, except for the highway between us, and life went on.

In those days, all our family members were still close by: Norma and Cal and kids just across the road; Kirk and Gunn just eighteen miles up the road at Kathleen Lake, with their little daughter Tanya; and Ted, Connie, and their brand new baby Roxanne in the middle, ten miles away at Cortino Lodge.

When the Kluane National Park borders were expanded, the Canadian government offered to buy Cal's acreage and home as housing for one of the park wardens, so and he and Norma moved to Whitehorse again. Cal had previously been employed with the Canadian Broadcasting Company for about fifteen years. He has an exceptionally pleasant and expressive speaking voice, and a gift with words that made him a natural for announcing on the radio. He had worked up to the job of producer before the urge to do something different hit him and they had bought the lodge. Now he got his former job with CBC back.

He and Norma bought a duplex in Whitehorse, one in a row of Steelox buildings in Hillcrest, the area that used to be occupied by the U.S. Air Force. When the Air Force moved from Whitehorse, all the buildings went to Canadian War Assets; and now they were for sale.

14

Challenge to Be Free

Going back now to a day in 1968, shortly after we turned the lodge over to Norma and Cal, we returned from a weekend in Whitehorse to be greeted by the news that Jimmy Kane had become a movie star.

A producer by the name of Chuck Keen, who owned Alaska Pictures Inc., had taken him off to Juneau, Alaska. Chuck was around thirty years old at the time, a former logger from southeastern Alaska who had turned to camera work; he had also become a successful freelance writer. He had shot seventeen films for the U.S. Army on the Vietnam war, and one on the disastrous Alaska earthquake.

Chuck had met Ward Beebe through his association with the Walt Disney Studios and hired him to direct *The Alaska Boy*, a feature film that Chuck was producing at the time. It was filmed in Alaska by Alaskans, and the star of the film was a twelve-year-old Tlinget boy, Tony Williams.

Chuck had seen an article with a full-page picture of Jimmy Kane's face, which Cal Waddinton had sent in to the *Alaska Sportsman.*

"Is this man still around here?" he asked Cal.

"Sure is. He's over at his cabin right now."

"Well, he looks just like the actor I've been looking for to take the part of Tony's grandfather in my movie."

When Cal took him over to meet Jimmy, Chuck was convinced.

"The man's a natural for the part. He'll fill the bill perfectly."

His trained eye had recognized the photogenic quality in Jimmy's face, and he was drawn to his natural charm and congenial manner. He was struck by Jimmy's resemblance to Chief Dan George.

168

Jimmy was quite contented with his lifestyle, but after pondering the idea for some time, he agreed to take the role. Until that time, he had never been any farther from home than Whitehorse. It turned out to be quite an exciting experience for him; still, he took it all in his stride, with his usual philosophical attitude.

Several times during the filming, Jimmy was able to come back home to Dezadeash Lake for a break. During these periods, he would stock up on gophers, which he hung by their necks to cure, until it was time to go back to Juneau. Then he'd put them in a gunny sack, throw them over his shoulder, and ride the bus to Haines, Alaska. Before boarding the ferry to Juneau, he'd distribute these gophers to his friends in Haines. They were a treat for the friends, but not for the bus passengers, who had to put up with the foul odor of the ripe animals until they had reached their destination. On one of these filming breaks, Jimmy arrived back home sporting his first pair of sunglasses.

"How does it feel to be a movie star now, Jimmy?" Gordon asked him.

"Oh well," he replied, "guess everybody in WHOLE WORLD sees me now, eh?"

In 1971, the *Alaska Boy* being completed, Chuck decided to make another film, based on the book, *The Saga of the Mad Trapper of Rat River,* written by Dick North. This is probably the best researched and most authentic chronicle of the chase ever written.

The true identity of the trapper, Albert Johnson, was never established for certain, but the imaginations of people all over the world were sparked by the dramatic manhunt launched by the Royal Canadian Mounted Police after he had killed one Mountie and wounded two others. The story was top news in all the major newspapers across the land. The hunt started at the beginning of 1932 and lasted for fifty-four torturous days, when a posse of Mounted Police, dog mushers, and guides set out to bring Johnson back, dead or alive—and succeeded.

An extremely powerful man, the trapper was also wily and resolute. Although the temperature at the time hovered between forty and fifty below zero, he outwitted and outran them all, until

169

the fatal mistake that cost him his life. This historical event took place along the Yukon–Northwest Territories boundary. Chuck wanted to re-create it in the southwestern Yukon, in the spectacular St. Elias mountain range near Dezadeash.

The movie was eventually called *Challenge to be Free*, and the trapper was portrayed by Mike Mazurki, a rugged Hollywood actor and ex-wrestler who has played in 125 motion pictures and even more television shows.

Chuck approached Gordon to help him scout out the best locations, to assist with moving the equipment and movie crews around to different spots, plus various other jobs that would be required. Besides the Hollywood actors, he hired local Yukoners to take parts, including a couple of friends of ours, Alex Van Bibber and Bob McKinnon. Gordon also had a part, and our son Ted was production manager, doubling as assistant photographer, and shooting many scenes in the film.

Jim and Buela Cortino offered their lodge as a base for the crews to work out of, and a place for them to live for the duration of the shooting. It was an ideal location and situation for everyone concerned.

For this movie, Chuck included Tay Garnet, the veteran director of John Wayne's early films. Tay's glamorous young wife was along; the plan originally was to have her take a part, but in the end hers was one of the scenes cut during the final edit. Ward Beebe worked with Chuck again, and, of course, he had to have Jimmy Kane as Old Tracks, the Indian scout who planned the strategy of the epic chase by the police to bring in Albert Johnson, the mad trapper.

Chuck contacted the RCMP for assistance in obtaining uniforms for the movie, and in having members of the force as actors; but he was turned down. He eventually had to accept an offer from the Alaska State Troopers to take the part of the Mounties. They were camouflaged quite well, though, because the parkas covered the uniforms and it was a small matter to add yellow stripes to the trousers.

The bear that Trapper wrestled in the film was the same one used in the "Grizzly Adams" television series. The old wolf, Trapper's companion, was in reality half Husky, half wolf, and

170

belonged to an elderly man who had recently built a cabin close to our hay meadow.

The lynx that Trapper found in his cabin one day, and befriended, actually was a wild one that Ted had kept for weeks in the lodge basement. Ted had been trying to tame the beast but no amount of pampering, feeding, and attention could improve that wildcat's disposition. It would spit and snarl whenever anyone tried to approach it. One day, someone neglected to hook the door of the cage properly after feeding the animal. The next time Ted opened the basement door, it was outside in a flash, and in a split second had leaped high up into a tree, hissing and baring its fangs.

Ted stood there looking up at the lynx in dismay, wondering how in the world he could capture it again. They needed this critter rather badly for the movie. Suddenly he had a brainwave. By this time, one of the lodge employees had come out to join him, and Ted yelled, "Quick! Run and get me a sleeping bag."

"A sleeping bag? What are you going to do, camp under the tree until he comes down?"

"Just GET it, quick!"

Minutes later, he was climbing the tree, sleeping bag around his shoulders. He threw it over the lynx, and then and there all hell broke loose. Trying to hold onto the animal inside the bag, and still keep his grip on the tree, proved to be impossible, and in the process he lost his footing and down fell Ted, the lynx, and the sleeping bag into the snow.

Fortunately, he fell right on top of the animal, which was still struggling to get out from under the bag, but trying to keep a grip on it was not easy. It squirmed around in there so fast that the minute Ted thought he had one end of the bag wrapped around the animal tightly, a head would appear out the other end; and when he'd throw the bag over the head, its hind feet would thrash out from below. Feathers from the torn bag were flying all over the place. The language Ted was using he had NOT learned at home, but finally, sweating and lunging around in the snow, he managed to get the beast under control.

Back again in the cage, the wildcat continued to hiss and snarl, in spite of all the good food and affection heaped upon it.

Watching it perform in the film, we secretly smiled, knowing that the good-natured, mild animal portrayed there had been tranquilized. It was positively mellow.

When the movie was completed, Ted was only too happy to send it to a zoo in the States that wanted it.

As Gordon and I were living just ten miles from the Cortino Lodge, we would drive over every morning to take part in the day's activities. The weather cooperated beautifully, and even though the temperature dropped way down at nights, the days were bright and sunny, with cloudless blue skies. We would all pile into the large van with our lunches and drive out to location where the day's shooting was taking place. Never having seen a movie being made before, we found it to be a very exciting and heady experience.

These were times I will never forget. The weather was ideal, just below freezing, and we were filming some of the most beautiful winter scenes in existence. There was a scene in the script that had to be filmed in a blizzard, with the trapper struggling through the wind and snow. Day after day went by, and still the weather remained perfect—no wind in a clear blue sky. Chuck was faced with the challenge of improvising a fake blizzard—somehow. Between Gordon, Ted, and Chuck, they came up with the idea of using the propeller of an airboat for a powerful fan, into which they could shovel snow and create an artificial storm. The airboat was brought up from Haines, Alaska, where the owner had been using it on the Chilkoot River. The men hauled it out on the frozen lake where the snow was deep.

It did the job quite well. About six of us had shovels, and when Chuck yelled "Shoot!" we'd shovel like mad, throwing the snow into the fan. It was a difficult scene to shoot, however, and they had to do quite a few "takes" of it. By the time Mike Mazurki had struggled through the storm half a dozen times on his snowshoes, falling down again and again and wiping the wet snow from his face, I think his good nature was tried almost to the breaking point.

One by one, the dog teams had to follow him through the blizzard. By the time it was all over, our arms felt like they'd fall off from shoveling all that snow. A hot drink from the thermos

172

bottles restored everyone's strength and we returned to Cortino Lodge, where the cook had a hot meal waiting for us.

Two or three times a week, a courier would arrive with the "rushes," the film that had been sent out for processing. These were very eagerly awaited, and we'd sit around in the lobby in a circle, watching them on the screen. It was clear to see that this film was going to be a success. When I saw the final film, I was disappointed at the number of scenes we had watched of the "rushes" that had been, of necessity, cut out. Even so, it was a popular film, being held over time and again at theaters all across Canada and the States. When it was adapted for television, unfortunately, it had to be cut some more.

Four dog teams were brought in from Fairbanks, Alaska, for the film, mostly trained Siberian Huskies. They were all strong young dogs, straining at their harnesses, yapping and whining, anxious to run. Alex Van Bibber, who took the part of the top sharpshooter in the posse, mushed his own team.

A longtime friend of ours, Bob McKinnon, was one of the mushers; Gordon, as a supply officer, also had a team in the posse. He wore a red headband and a Hudson's Bay jacket, white, with red, black, green, and yellow stripes. Another team was handled by the owner of the dogs, and the fifth by a Hollywood actor.

The lead sleigh was reserved for Jimmy Kane, or Old Tracks, who gave the directions with a wave of his hand. He was the favorite of the whole crew.

Our son, Ted, was blown away with a blast from Trapper's gun. Portraying a brassy young rookie, he had marched up to Trapper's cabin, pounded on the door, and demanded that Trapper come out. At the same moment as the blast went off, an invisible piano wire tied to his waist was yanked back by a couple of men behind the camera, jerking Ted back into a prone position in the snow. It was so realistic I almost fainted.

One afternoon, when everyone was killing time between scenes, Mike Mazurki pushed me around in an empty dog sleigh.

"I'll bet you could even push me," he teased. Mike is a big man, probably over 200 pounds, but I pushed him with no effort on the snow that day. I was amazed at how easy it was on the frozen snow. Someone snapped a picture of us, which I will always treasure.

There was one scene that was cut out in *Challenge to be Free* that I really felt should have been left in. It showed Jimmy Kane standing on a hill over his brother's "Spirit House." The snow was up to his knees and he was silhouetted against the blue sky, chanting a eulogy to the memory of his brother.

In the silence of the cold clear air, the sound of his voice was electrifying, the wavering, guttural sounds seeming to come from the depths of his soul and rising up into the sky. After a while, Chuck lowered his camera and said, "Okay—Cut." But Jimmy never heard a thing.

He had his head up and his eyes closed, carried away to a spiritual world of his own. Nothing was going to stop him until he had finished that song.

Home Town Again

In 1974, Kirk and Gunn sold Kathleen Lake Lodge and moved to Whitehorse with our little granddaughters, Tanya and Naomi. Ted was already renting a house there—he and Connie had unfortunately gone their separate ways by this time, a couple of kids who really were too young for the responsibility of managing a lodge, and trying to raise a little girl at the same time. Jim Cortino had put the lodge up for sale.

It was getting pretty lonesome in our house on the meadow, with all our family so far away now. We made arrangements to lease the hay meadow to Rod Tait and move to Whitehorse ourselves. We could still drive out on weekends, we reasoned, but there just wasn't enough activity around now to stay on permanently at Dezadeash.

The day before we left stands out in my mind. It was a hot one. When it had cooled a bit in the late afternoon, I took a walk down to the edge of the lake. The sun's rays were still warm on the back of my neck, but the breeze coming over the water had a refreshing coolness. I walked out on the old wooden wharf and sat down on the edge, dangling my feet in the water. The only sounds to be heard were the little waves slap-slapping against the weathered pilings, and somewhere, way in the distance, an outboard motor was starting up.

I sat there a long time, just thinking and enjoying the solitude, letting the tensions melt away. I had been packing all day, a job I had never enjoyed.

'How peaceful it is here,' I thought. 'I wonder what's in store for us now? I hope we won't be sorry.'

We bought a Steelox duplex alongside Norma and Cal in Whitehorse, and Gordon and Kirk formed a construction company, which they called St. Elias Enterprises.

There was a building boom going on at the time and new housing was going up like mad in Riverdale. The developers needed somebody to do the excavating and cement work for basements and foundations, and Gordon and Kirk won the bid for one of the contracts that were let out. They also hauled topsoil, gravel, and anything else that needed hauling. They both bought Kenworth trucks, and eventually acquired Cats, loaders, and cement mixers.

A year later, Gordon and I sold off the Steelox duplex and built a home in the subdivision of Hillcrest. Our address was Number 2, Sunset Drive North. This was our home for the next eleven years, even though we were away during much of the time.

It was there that we bought our first television set and, for the first time in our married life, I had all kinds of time on my hands. Too much time!

I found it very hard to adjust to the life in Whitehorse after all those years at Dezadeash. It was the first time I wasn't actively participating in our means of livelihood, and instead of enjoying the leisure time as I had expected to do, I became dejected.

Norma came over one day and said, "Mom, why don't you try your hand at painting? You might like it, you know. I know a girl who's taking Ted Harrison's course at the Vocational School, and she really likes it. You're not the type to sit around and drink tea with the ladies in the afternoon, or play bridge, and it's not good for you to be at loose ends like this."

"Well, it's a thought. Maybe I'll phone and see if there's an opening."

The next day I found out that they did have room for me as someone had dropped out. The only problem was, two months had already gone by in the four-month course. I went down and registered anyway.

A whole new world was suddenly opened up to me. The art center in the school was a new student's delight, with a variety of fascinating choices of things to learn that made one's head spin, and all under the excellent direction of Ted Harrison.

There was a very relaxed atmosphere of camaraderie in this classroom, and everyone seemed to be really excited and interested in learning their particular skills.

The students were working at silk screening, sketching, calligraphy, wood carving, clay sculpting, watercoloring, oil painting, drawing in pen and ink, and painting with acrylics. And over in one corner of the large room were the potters, sitting at the electric pottery wheels, or kneading and rolling out clay on the long wooden tables.

Each project I watched seemed more fascinating than the one before; but I had come here to get some instruction on sketching, and I would have to restrict myself to that—for the time being at least.

Every day, though, I would find myself being irresistibly drawn to the potters' wheels. There was a sort of magic about the way that wet lump of clay could be coaxed into useful items, such as vases and bowls.

'Back to the sketching table,' I would scold myself. 'Try to exercise some restraint.'

But, time and again, I'd find myself back at the pottery section, gazing mesmerized at the lucky people at the wheels.

"Why don't you try it yourself?" asked a voice behind me one day. There was never any mistaking that voice with the British accent.

"You mean it's all right?"

"Of course it is! Sit down here and I'll give you a bit of a lesson."

"I think you have a flair for pottery," Ted told me the next day. "If that's what you want to do, go ahead—whatever's the most fun for you."

176

I had found my niche. One thing I liked about this craft was the fact that there was never any doubt whether you were doing something the right or the wrong way. Clay will not permit incorrect handling—it will just collapse or flatten itself out in no uncertain terms. Sometimes, though, if you hadn't been too blatantly insensitive but were starting to squeeze a bit too hard, the clay would give a gentle warning, by beginning to wobble on the wheel. If you were lucky, you could change your tactics before all was lost and your pot turned into a flat pancake.

Ted also taught us the art of glazing, and about the materials that were used in the process. Now I was completely hooked!

When the course was finished, I searched around and found someone who made and sold pottery wheels, and had him install one in our basement. Then I sent away to Vancouver for a kiln, and loads of material for glazing. Gordon installed a sink in my corner of the room, built cupboards for all the paraphernalia that is required for this hobby, and I was in business.

Now he could go off digging basements and hauling gravel knowing that I was content. Not only content, but utterly addicted. I would glaze a batch of pots in the afternoon and place them carefully in the kiln. They looked like they were covered with dull mud, dutifully waiting for their baptism by fire. It would be the next morning before the kiln would be cool enough to raise the lid. If you peeked too soon, I discovered to my sorrow one day, the pots could crack from the sudden temperature change.

Now, when I woke up in the morning, I would leap out of bed and run downstairs. I would stand there for a minute by the kiln, cross my fingers and close my eyes for a minute, then slowly raise the lid. There they would be—my creations—in all their vibrant rainbow of glory.

Sometimes an indignant voice from the kitchen would bring me back to earth again: "Hey, where's my breakfast?" But it was with a feeling of fulfilment that I'd bound upstairs to put the coffee on.

I enjoyed my pottery for a couple of years, and sold enough at the Spruce-bog Fair, which the craft society used to organize a couple of times a year, to pay for my hobby and keep the basement shelves from overflowing. Then, unfortunately, I developed

177

an allergy to the clay and had to give it up because my hands kept breaking out in a rash.

By this time, though, the building boom had subsided somewhat, so we had more time to traipse around the country.

15

Why Not Try Gold Mining?

Prospecting and mining for gold has always held a certain fascination for Gordon. Whenever we had some spare time over the years, we would drive the 110 miles to Atlin, B.C., and spend a day hiking around the creeks where the old-timers had mined during the Klondkie Gold Rush.

There was a fair amount of activity going on in 1977 due to the increased price of gold. It was around this time that we became acquainted with Karl Siegar, who had a small placer operation on Pine Creek, just seven miles east of Atlin. His cabin was on the old townsite of Discovery, where the first gold in the are was discovered in 1896.

A few of the original buildings remained in various stages of decay, some of them barely hanging on—nostalgic reminders of an era long since past. For nearly ninety years, winter blizzards and howling north winds had battered away at them. Each spring, though, the grass would green on the sagging sod roofs, and wild raspberry bushes, crocuses, and fireweed would bring life to the old log walls, as if by nurturing them in this way they would be encouraged to stand up for a while longer. With a little restoration, some of the sturdier cabins were made habitable, though, and it was in one of these that Karl lived.

His wife, Thelma, worked in Whitehorse; she came out on weekends, laden with pies and home cooking. If Karl had a "cleanup" since her last visit, she would take the gold back to Whitehorse for safekeeping in the bank.

Gordon liked to go down to the sluicebox and help Karl, for something to do, and I'd sit in the kitchen and watch Thelma clean the gold, as we called it. Sometimes I'd give her a hand. The method she used seemed very slow and tedious to me, but apparently all the miners there did it the same way; one of the larger outfits at the time even hired unemployed women from town to come out on cleanup days to process the gold in this same manner.

Karl and Thelma never seemed to bother with the flour gold, although it was certainly there. Karl would pick the larger nuggets right out of the sluicebox, as they are usually near the top, and put them into a tobacco can. Then he'd pan the concentrates, as they called the muck they shoveled out of the box during a cleanup; it was a mixture of fine gravel, sand, and gold. When he was through with the panning, Karl would have the stuff concentrated down to roughly a gallon pailful. From there on, it was women's work, he said.

Thelma and I would spoon this concentrate onto sheets of white paper and clean it little by little, hour after hour. Once I had caught on to the job, I found it intriguing to watch our small jars gradually filling up with the shiny little pieces of gold, which ranged in size from almost sugarlike particles to as big as my thumbnail.

There was always a quantity of heavy black sand mixed with the gold, most of which was magnetite—and therefore magnetic—so the trick was to use a small magnet to lift it off the paper, leaving only the light sand, small pebbles, and gold. The very fine sand would have to be carefully blown off, the rest picked and pushed aside. Finally, there would be nothing left but a little pile of the yellow metal, and we'd fold the paper into a funnel and slide the little bit of treasure into the jars.

This was my initiation into how I'd be spending a lot of summer days during the next fourteen years.

The mine was a quarter mile down the road from the cabins. Karl was digging in an old creek bottom with his Cat, pushing the overburden up into piles, which grew daily until they became too steep for the Cat; then he'd start another one. When he was down to about a foot above bedrock, it was time to start putting the gravel through the sluicebox. Karl would shovel it into the hopper at the top end, where water under pressure from a pump he had set up on Pine Creek would wash it on down the steel sluicebox, which was secured to a ramp Karl and some helpers had built on a slope. The box was lined with heavy burlap sacking,

180

over which a grid of expanded steel mesh was placed in sections, and the gravel, sand, and boulders were washed down over this. During this sluicing, the gold dropped through the mesh onto the burlap, where it became trapped on the bottom; it very seldom moved from there. Karl always hoped it would all get hung up in the top third of the box. Once in a while, though, especially if the box was too full and became packed with too much clay, it would ride up and over the end of the box, which is what all good miners seek to avoid. Many a nugget has been found in old tailing piles where this has apparently happened.

Sometimes Karl worked alone, but more often he would have another man helping him. Someone would have to be the "rock puller" in that type of operation, as large boulders would sometimes get hung up or jammed together while being washed down the sluice. They used a long-handled, two-pronged fork to reach in and release them. This was a tiring and sometimes strenuous job, keeping the men on their feet all day long. The rock puller doubled as a tailing man. This job consisted of clearing the rocks and debris—tailings—from the base of the sluicebox, where they continuously build up in the water. A bucket loader is used for this purpose, picking up the washed rocks and gravel and carrying them off to a tailing pile.

These tailing piles differed from the ones left by the old-timers, as in the early days most of them were formed by hand work—using picks and shovels—and consisted of clean rocks with very little sand and soil mixed with them.

Another type of tailings common to Atlin and Dawson City are the ones left by the earlier giant dredges, row after row of uniform mounds snaking across the land for miles and miles.

I used to think the bare piles of rocks were ugly and desolate. They were always there—they were my view when I'd gaze out the window in the evenings. In time though, I found myself falling under their spell. 'If they could only talk,' I thought, 'the stories they could tell!' I began to notice that in addition to being ever-present, they were also ever-changing. A few persistent little green trees and numerous wildflowers would start to flourish around the bases of these piles in the spring. After a rain, the wetness of the rocks would sparkle in the sunlight, and in the evening they would form silhouettes against the sunset. Then, on a cold fall morning, just the tops would show above the slowly vanishing fog.

'Why, they're beautiful.' I thought. 'How could I ever have thought them ugly?'

When cleanup day arrived, Karl would shut off the water and take the box apart. We didn't actually see this part of the operation until later in the summer, after we had bought Karl's property and did it ourselves for the first time.

Karl Siegar was suffering from a bad back, and the work was becoming harder for him all the time, so he decided to sell the property and go out of the mining business.

Back in Whitehorse, I had just thrown a ball of fresh clay on my wheel and was starting to pull it up into a slippery wet teapot when Gordon came in the back door. It was just before I had made the decision that I'd have to give up pottery for a while because of my hands.

"Hi, are you home?" he called.

"I'm in the basement working on my pottery," I replied. He came downstairs.

"You're not ready, yet? I thought we were going to Atlin. I have to give Karl an answer today on that property."

"Are you really serious about this?" I asked him. "It's a pretty big move to make, you know."

"Well," Gordon said, "we've tried a lot of projects in our day, they all worked out okay. Why NOT go gold mining?"

'Here we go again,' I thought, and went over to the sink to wash my hands.

Driving over the gravel road to Atlin an hour later, I watched Little Atlin Lake slowly drifting by. 'It would be nice to live around Atlin for the summer,' I mused.

"I wonder if Harold and Rita Olson would be interested in going in with us," said Gordon. "I think he's at loose ends right now."

"Well, it won't hurt to ask them."

By this time I was excited at the prospect of mining, and we decided we'd buy the property, even if we did it on our own. Harold and Rita were in favor of going into a partnership, however, so in July of 1978 we signed an agreement with Karl for the six claims and property, and moved to Discovery for the mining season.

I'll never forget our first cleanup. After sluicing for a week, the men decided it was time. But nothing had prepared us for how long this hard, back-breaking job was going to take. Extra help was not available just then, so Rita and I pitched in. Like everything else, there is a right and a wrong way to do a job, and with all four of us being as green as grass that first time, I guess we chose the hard way. At any rate, once we'd removed the expanded steel sections and could see little pieces of gold exposed to view, we didn't feel we could leave it until the job was finished.

We shut off the water from the main pipeline now, and did the finishing with a smaller pump and handheld hose. We washed and washed the remaining material in the box, then washed and washed some more. Then we had to remove all the heavy burlap and put it in tubs of water, to be rinsed out later. Next, we raked down the bare riffles, and washed some more.

"There's a big nugget," cried Rita.

"Oh, look, here's another," I yelled.

"All right, girls, up off your bellies and back on your feet. There's lots of work to be done here."

"Aw, you're no fun at all!"

Finally we had the balance of the concentrates shoveled into five-gallon pails, and loaded onto the back of the pickup beside the tubs of wet burlap sacking.

Eight hours had elapsed since we started; we'd even forgotten to have lunch. Exhausted by then, we threw down our shovels and lay down flat on the ground, not moving or even thinking, for about twenty minutes. Finally, one by one, we started to stir, got up, looked at each other, and started to laugh. We all began talking at once.

"Looked pretty good, eh?"

"We'll know more when we get those mats washed."

"Who's going to pan out all those pails of concentrate?"

"Why, you ladies of course."

"That's no job for a lady. Karl used to do it."

Gordon spoke up. "Yes, but Harold and I have to put the box together and start sluicing again. Say, how about some dinner? I'm starved."

"Well, you gold addicts can just buy us dinner in town tonight, then. I'm not cooking, are you, Rita?"

"Huh! Not on you're life."

"You two can't go looking like that, can you?"

"Just watch us!"

Nothing could dampen our spirits that night. We rinsed our faces in the cold stream, threw a canvas over the back of the pickup, and took the car into Atlin. We parked outside the Inn and walked into the cafe. We sat at a table, blissfully ignoring our grimy clothes and the puzzled stares of a few local people, not to mention the waitress. They must have been wondering why we never cleaned ourselves up, especially before dining on steaks and wine, and why that look of jubilation on our faces? They had no way of knowing how new we were to this game.

And how much we did learn over the years.

The Second Phase

Gordon and Harold washed out the burlap mats the next day and put the resultant concentrate into more pails, freeing up the tubs so Rita and I could fill them with clean water and start working.

I would start panning and when my back hurt, she would spell me off. Then I could dry the stuff I had panned out. This was accomplished by putting it in a beat-up old gold pan and setting it on low heat on the propane burner of the kitchen stove. It would have to be stirred until bone dry, then dumped onto the sheets of white paper on the table. We would both work at this for a while, then start the procedure all over again. It took us about five days of steady work, between cooking and dishes, until we had it all cleaned, weighed up on the gold scales, and labeled in glass jars.

Gunn and Kirk used to come out from Whitehorse on week-ends and give us a very welcome hand. Gunn would pitch right in and she became a real whiz at panning and cleaning. After a time, they joined us as third partners, and Kirk brought out his two scrapers—huge earth-moving buggies used for roadwork—rented one out, and used the other for removing overburden on our property. They moved into Karl's old cabin, fixed it up with new linoleum and curtains, and put their two girls, Tanya and Naomi, into the Atlin school.

With a third hand in the cleaning process, we even had time to do some antique-bottle digging.

Karl was a high-strung, explosive man, and wanted no strangers interfering with his life. He had kept the groups of ardent bottle hunters off his property in all the years he'd been mining there. A lot of the old dumps in surrounding areas had been ransacked many times over the years, but one day we discovered, right under the spot where Karl had been throwing his empty cans, that there was a bonanza of precious bottles from the gold rush days. What an exciting find! From then on, we were hooked —addicted, in fact, to digging and collecting.

We became quite expert in ferreting out the old dumps. We would prepare the men's lunches, leave them on the table, and off to the woods we would go, our picks and shovels and garden tools tucked under our arms. When they went home to an empty cabin at noon, all the men would have to do was to listen closely and they could hear the distant sounds of broken bottles being flung over a bank, shovels hitting on glass and rocks, and shrieks coming from the nearby woods.

"Come quickly! I've found a beauty."

"I can't, I'm in a really good spot."

"Over here! There's millions of them."

At the end of the day we'd traipse home, flushed with success and covered with mud and dirt from head to toe, reeking of mosquito dope and sweat, lugging our sacks of treasures over our shoulders.

"Is this any way for grandmothers to be acting?" Gordon would ask.

I think we worked harder than the men. After all that digging, we'd have to haul water from the creek, fill up the tubs, and wash our precious collection. This was no easy task, as anyone who has tried to clean a hundred years of accumuled mud, silt, and leaves

185

out of a bottle can testify. Amazingly enough, though, we found some that were immaculate, usually in the deep moss, and some very delicate ones, too.

One year, Gunn and I had more than 500 bottles between us, all washed, labeled, catalogued, and packed into cardboard boxes. In the fall, we lugged them into our basements in Whitehorse. I sold a few boxfuls to a collector, kept some of my favorite small bottles, and gave the rest to Gunn. I think they're still in her basement today.

Looking back, now, I realize that all this digging must have been during a period when the men were stripping and stockpiling at the mine because when we were in production and sluicing, the women certainly didn't have much time for frivolities such as bottle digging. What with bookkeeping, cooking and baking for the crew, shopping in town for supplies, and doing the laundry there, plus the never-ending gold cleaning, there wasn't much time left for anything.

When berry season came around, though, the can opener came into its own for a week or two while we picked berries and made our own jams and jellies. It was a good life, even with the hard work and the short mining season.

The high for gold in the year we started mining was $249.80 a troy ounce in U.S. funds. A level teaspoonful of the finest weighed one troy ounce, so there was money in it. But expenses in a mining camp can be phenomenal, even with good management, and especially if you're unlucky enough to have a breakdown in equipment.

I remember being shocked when a drive went in our D-8 Cat and Gordon told me it would cost $15,000 to replace. Nowadays it would probably be a lot more. All our men being good mechanics helped to keep our down time to a minimum. Even so, the bulk of what we made went back into the operation.

We upgraded all the equipment, went from our basic gravity sluicebox to a large, modern (by comparison) Pierson box with a big spray bar. Then we substituted the heavy sacking for the newer green artificial turf that most miners were using. It made a huge difference in the time spent on cleanups, being lighter and much easier to wash out.

186

In the next year or two, we created quite a little community at Discovery. At one point, we had six families there, in cabins and trailers, where there had only been the Siegars before. Our son Ted and his family joined us; our littlest grandson, Arkell, was just a baby then. Rita and Harold had their son Buddy and his family there, and Harold's sister and brother-in-law, Lorraine and Nick, came up from California. We had some good times together, although the social life was starting to compete a bit with the hours the men wanted to put into mining.

Later on, Harold and Gordon agreed that there was enough property and equipment for two mining operations. So we split everything down the middle. Our family took three claims and Harold's the other three. We gave Harold the first choice, then took turns on the others. So instead of partners, we became neighbors, each group with its own operation.

I loved having the family, with the grandchildren, close by all summer. To see Norma and Cal, though, we would have to go to Whitehorse. We could check up on our empty house there at the same time.

By this time, Norma and Cal were operating—and still do—a thriving audiovisual business by the name of A.V. Action, Ltd., and were producing films and documentaries for private firms and organizations wanting to advertise, for the CBC, and for various governmental departments such as tourism and environment.

Cal's years of experience in production with CBC, coupled with his own natural talent in narration and writing, proved to be a valuable asset. So was Norma's expertise in photography, which she loves. She spent many happy hours building up a large library of resource and reference slides for the business. Kurt and Kris had both graduated from high school now; Kurt was off to college, and Kris had a secretarial job in Whitehorse.

When the ground started to freeze, and too much ice was forming in the sluicebox, we would move back to Whitehorse.

After Christmas, Gordon and I would pack up and head south to California or Mexico, driving the Alaska Highway as we had done every year since it was built. As much as we enjoyed these times, the best part was always getting back home in the beginning of March, usually when the snowmobiling and skiing was at its best.

The Unforseen Happens

When bad luck did come, it struck with a vengeance.

There were still a few patches of virgin ground between the old tailing piles on our property which the early miners had missed. There could be rich spots underneath some of those piles, too, because the old-timers, having to start their mining somewhere and begin sluicing, would have to dump the first overburden on unmined ground; it was anyone's guess where they had started their digging. We started looking for those rich spots.

Gordon enjoyed hiking over those tailing piles, trying to envision the lay of the land as it may have been in the early days and speculating about where the old creek beds used to run before the water was diverted into new channels.

He came home for lunch one day after one of these hikes late in July, 1981, and after eating, he lay down for a nap on the couch. Our little Chihuahua, Freddy, curled up on his chest, as usual, and went to sleep. It was around one o'clock in the afternoon. Half an hour later, as I was washing the lunch dishes at the kitchen sink, I heard the dog jump to the floor and Gordon saying in a deep, garbled-sounding voice, "Well, Fred, we'd better get back to work." He always enjoyed teasing Freddy, and I thought that was what he was doing then. I wondered vaguely why Gordon was dragging his feet as he walked past me into the bathroom. I figured he must still be half asleep. He spoke again from the bathroom, but I couldn't make out the words. When he came out again, I was still busy at the sink. He was saying something, still in that unnatural voice. Half irritated that he was keeping this game up so long, I turned and started to say, "I can't hear what you are saying," but I stopped, shocked at his appearance.

"I—think—I—have—a—problem."

It was an effort for him to get the words out. His face looked lopsided, and his right arm hung limply at his side. A wave of terror threatened to engulf me; my throat became bone dry and

188

my heart began pounding. For a second or two, I couldn't speak; my voice was gone.

'DON'T PANIC! *Stay calm,*' I told myself, trying to blot out the other thoughts that rushed to my mind. I persuaded Gordon to lie down on the couch again.

"It's all right," I told him, "you'll be fine. I'll get Ted."

There was no one in camp except the two of us. Everyone else was either at the mine, a quarter mile down the road, or in Whitehorse. Incredibly, there was a sound outside, which made me glance out the window. I saw Bo, just as he rode his bike past our trailer. Bo was about ten years old, one of the three children who lived with their parents in an old log cabin about half a mile down the road toward Atlin. I ran out and stopped him.

"Go to the mine and get Ted just as quickly as you can, Bo," I said. "Don't stop for anything. Mr. Yardley's had a stroke!"

I came back in and started stuffing some clothes into a bag to take to town, and in a few minutes Ted's car was screeching to a stop outside the door. We helped Gordon into the back seat and headed for Whitehorse. It was a nightmarish ride. Ted's face was white, and he was breaking all speed records getting to town. "Don't have—to—hurry—on my ac—count," came Gordon's voice from the back seat. His attempt at humor was lost on us as we were too scared to appreciate it. But Ted smiled anyway, and said, "We're not going on a 'joy ride,' Dad." Even at the speed we were traveling, though, it seemed to take forever to get to Whitehorse.

Gordon woke up when we got there and wanted us to take him right to our house. He was very insistent that we not go to the hospital first, in spite of our arguments. Feeling dazed, as if in the midst of a bad dream, I followed them into the house. Suddenly, all our kids were there; everyone was trying to convince Gordon that he must go to the hospital. Making his way to the bathroom by himself, he closed the door, shutting us all out in the hall. When I thought he had been in there long enough, I went in to see if he was all right. He was standing at the mirror, trying to shave with his old safety razor. He had cut himself in several places but when I reached up to help, he just brushed my hand out of the way and carried on, determined. I turned away and left the room before he could see the tears in my eyes. I walked into our bedroom, sobbing. This was more than I could bear; my proud, independent, strong husband—always in control—struck down like a helpless child. Knowing this was not the time to break down, I choked back the tears with great effort and went into the kitchen to heat some soup for him. Gordon wouldn't let anyone help him eat it, even though the spoon kept falling out of his hand. Someone was making phone calls. Everything seemed unreal. Kirk and Ted finally had to take their dad firmly by the arm, one on each side, and help him into the car.

"You don't have to come, Mom," Ted said. "Stay and get some rest—you're tired out."

"Are you serious?" I answered, climbing into the back seat with Gordon.

By the next day, the doctor had Gordon's blood pressure partly under control. Kirk and Ted went back to Atlin to carry on for the remainder of the mining season.

We didn't know how long Gordon would be in the hospital. His right hand was practically useless now, and his speech was very slurred. The worst part of all, though, was the frustration he suffered. He would accept no sympathy, even from me, and I would sit there hour after hour by his bedside trying, in vain, to cheer him up. A hug would bring no response at all and I'd go home at the end of the day to our empty house feeling hurt and rejected. My heart felt as if it were breaking. It was as though he didn't want me or anyone else around.

"He has been dealt a hard blow; don't take it personally," the doctor told me. "This is a common reaction. Sometimes a personality change takes place after a stroke, but it doesn't always last."

I was not comforted. All the joy seemed to have gone out of life for me, but I knew that it had to be a lot worse for Gordon, and that it was vitally important for me to keep up a cheerful exterior.

Gordon stayed in the hospital for a week, greatly against his will. When he finally did come home, I had to do all the driving, among other things, for a few days. This was especially hard on Gordon's self-esteem and, probably long before he should have been, he was soon behind the wheel again. He kept exercising his

190

hand, but was very impatient that the progress he was making was so slow.

"Gordon, why don't we fly to Rochester and see if the doctors at the Mayo Clinic can help?" I suggested one day.

He thought it was worth a try. With the help of our doctor in Whitehorse, who gave us a referral, we were able to make the necessary arrangements. We flew to Rochester, Minnesota, where Gordon went through extensive tests at the clinic and ended up being hospitalized again, for a week, before they could get his blood pressure stabilized.

Back home again, the slow but steady process of recovery continued for Gordon. Little by little, the hard knot in my stomach began to go away. When he said to me, "I don't think I ever would have made it without your support," the knot disappeared entirely. It was the closest thing to sentiment I had heard in a long time.

16

Mining at Mount Freegold

The summer after his stroke, Gordon had improved to the point where he wanted to get back to work. His speech was almost normal again and, though he tired more quickly now, he was still able to live the life of a miner, which he enjoyed so very much.

I am eternally thankful our two sons were there to take over the business in Atlin during those first heartbreaking months while he was recuperating.

Like most miners in the area, we had replaced the Pierson box with a trommel, which is a huge horizontal drum about thirty feet long with the middle section perforated with three-quarter-inch holes about an inch apart. This is placed in a cradle, or frame, to raise it above the ground and hold it on a slight incline so the top end is higher. A strong steel hopper is built at the upper end, and water under pressure is piped into it. The drum itself is rotated continuously by an electric motor.

The man on the D-9 Cat, which was equipped with ripper teeth, stripped the overburden off, maybe half a mile away from where the trommel was located, and stockpiled the paydirt, which was picked up by the big scraper, or buggy. Then another Cat pushed the buggy and its load up to the trommel and dumped it. The backhoe operator then fed this material into the hopper, where the water washed it into the trommel. As the big drum turned, the smaller and heavier material would fall through the holes and onto the sluicebox, which was built right underneath. The larger boulders and slag would go out the bottom end into the settling pond; the loader man would carry the waste away to a tailing pile.

Finally, after moving tons and tons of earth this way, and the women had finished the panning out and drying, we would wind up—most nights—with a small jar of gold on the kitchen table. A small spice jar held fourteen troy ounces of gold. At roughly $670 per ounce, Canadian, which was the value of gold at one point that summer, that adds up to $9,380. Or, putting it another way, a beer bottle holds 100 ounces, at that time worth $67,000.

It wasn't long after that, though, that the price of gold dropped considerably.

One day in late August, 1983, while Gordon and I were having lunch in the Whitehorse Travelodge, a geologist friend of ours stopped by our table to visit. Ron Grainger had staked up most of Seymour Creek in the Mount Freegold area with a partner. He was looking for a reliable outfit to mine some of the claims there, about forty-five miles from Carmacks, on a percentage basis. He asked Gordon if he knew of anyone who might be interested.

Production on our own ground in Atlin had been starting to slow down lately, and although we hadn't yet exhausted all the potential, Gordon and Kirk were keeping an eye open for opportunities we could utilize in the future.

Ron was impatient for someone to take over right away. His partner had been working a portion of the property, but he decided to pull his equipment out when he encountered a large quantity of magnetite in the creek bottom; he found it too much of a problem to deal with. Ron, however, insisted that the paydirt was rich enough to warrant coping with the inconvenience.

Knowing Ron's reputation for honesty, Gordon agreed to go and have a look at it the next day. He gave Kirk, who was in Atlin, a rundown on the situation by phone. He came back to Whitehorse the following evening and phoned Kirk again, this time from Ron's house.

"What do you think about moving the equipment and crew to Freegold for the rest of the season? It doesn't look too bad to me."

That must have been what Kirk had hoped to hear, because he answered without any hesitation, "I think we can be on the road by tomorrow."

Gordon and I drove back to Atlin in our pickup, hooked up the Airstream trailer we had been living in that summer, and towed it to Seymour Creek. Some close friends of ours from California, Dixie and Lloyd Hall, came along with us. The Halls were self-contained in their own trailer and pickup. A retired couple who drove north to see our country, they ended up spending a couple of seasons with us, totally enjoying the experience, and in turn giving us the real pleasure of their company.

The magnetite turned out not to be a problem, and we mined there for the rest of that season and all the next summer.

Ron Grainger and his wife, Diane, were building a log cabin not far from where we had parked our trailer. There was a clear stream where we could catch grayling whenever we felt like it, and there were many wild cranberries, low bush blueberries, and red currants close by.

Kirk and Gunn set up their own trailer not far from ours. We rented the cookhouse that the previous outfit had used; it came complete with a spacious freezer and a cooking grill. We also rented the bunkhouse, a place for our crew of three men to sleep and shower. We brought in a large supply of food, and went to work.

Having started there so late in the season, it wasn't long before fall descended on us. The men decided that with five of them, they could work around the clock. That way they could keep the trommel turning over so the water couldn't freeze, and thereby extend the working season for a few extra weeks.

Previous to this, in Atlin, Ted had taken on a new venture of his own. He had come to Gordon one day with a suggestion:

"Dad," he said, "why don't you stake all this placer property for hardrock? At least the 'Yellow Jacket.' One of these days someone is going to do it, and it could be a problem for you if it turns out to be a stranger."

"Well, it's a good idea—why not do it yourself? Kirk and I don't really have the time right now."

Ted had been doing some research. He found that some of the ground we were working on was on the famous Yellow Jacket claim of the gold rush days. Such old claims were now being declared open, as the Crown grants had run out, so Ted staked our Yellow Jacket ground as hardrock claims and recorded them in Atlin. Hardrock is a type of mining where the ore is found in veins still embedded in the rock; placer mining is done where the associated rock and quartz has been eroded away, freeing the loose gold particles which then get washed by the rain into creek bottoms and crevices in the rocks. When a miner stakes a placer claim, he doesn't own the hardrock rights, and vice versa, unless he stakes it for that purpose also.

It wasn't long before Tri-West and Canova Resources became interested, and obtained an option on the property from Ted. He cashed in some of his shares and put the money into equipment, including a trommel and backhoe, and started his own mining operation on another creek in Atlin.

Then, in the last week of August, Gunn and Diane Grainger moved from Seymour Creek back to Whitehorse to get their kids back to school again, so I was the only woman left in camp.

It's hard for anyone who wasn't there to believe how hard the men all worked that fall at Seymour Creek. There weren't any complaints, even though they were eating and sleeping at crazy hours; they just seemed happy to be getting all those hours in, probably being well aware of a leaner winter season ahead. Every morning at five o'clock you could hear Tom or Arnie out there breaking ice in the creek so they could fill the barrel in the cookhouse with the day's supply of water. There can be no slackers in a mining camp; everyone has a job to do that depends on everyone else doing his.

I got to know all their favorite dishes; food becomes very important when you're out in the bush like that, with no television or any other entertainment available. We went through an awful lot of pies and cakes, gallons of hot, homemade soup and biscuits, chicken stew with dumplings, and freezerloads of meat. Kirk shot a young bull moose that fall, and the steaks from it were so tender that the men even ate them for breakfast; with lots of fresh cranberry sauce to go with them, they were a real treat.

It seemed like the meals and dishes just never ended, what with all the changing shifts. Then Gunn would arrive from Whitehorse for the weekend, and I think I was just as happy to see her as Kirk was. Not only did she pitch in and work like a trooper, but also it was just good to have a woman in camp to talk to. I'm sure there were lots of times she must have been weary from the long drive out, but she was always cheerful.

The next summer at Freegold was much more relaxed. We decided to do away with the cookhouse; Gunn cooked for her family when the kids were out of school, and I cooked for Gordon. We hired a man who brought his wife and trailer out, so they were self-contained, too. We ran only one regular shift, and we didn't need as much help now.

A little later in the summer, Ron Grainger wanted someone to work the claims below us. He phoned Ted, who was still in Atlin, and Ted ended up bringing his outfit to Seymour Creek, too. He was beginning to run out of paydirt in Atlin.

Suddenly there was a great burst of dust and activity, as all the vehicles started moving in. Included in the entourage was Ted's wife, Irena, our grandson, Arkell, who by now was going on four, and Ted's partners Rocky and Barbara. There were pickups pulling travel trailers; a big truck and loboy that Ted had hired to haul a Cat; the service truck that carries the tools and welder—a sort of a workshop on wheels; and another truck hauling the backhoe and loader. It was almost the identical setup that we had when we arrived there. So now we had two more families in camp.

Rocky was an American, a good-looking, dark-haired man with a stocky build and a mild and easygoing manner. He had come to the Yukon the year before and worked with a friend on Jarvis Creek. It was there he had met Ted, who happened to be doing some testing on the site. The two of them hit it off very well together, and Ted had talked him into working the Seymour claims with him.

Barbara

Rocky had met a girl from Australia when he came north. Barbara had blue eyes and long, blonde hair. She was a registered nurse on vacation at the time. She had intended to go back home to her job in a few weeks, but when she met Rocky her plans went by the wayside.

All of a sudden she wanted to go mining, too. At first we were all a bit skeptical that this slim, almost delicate-looking girl would last out the summer as a backhoe operator, but she turned out to be a lot tougher than we thought. Barbara sat up on the backhoe hour after hour, day after day, feeding the paydirt into the trommel.

So Ted had his crew for the summer. Irena did the cooking and they ate their meals in a large tent-frame, which the men constructed over a plank floor. They built a long table and benches, and it all made a brighter, roomier dining room than there was space for in the crowded trailer. It was also a good place to play cards in the evenings.

As is so often the case, it seems, the men, in time, became so accustomed to Barbara working the backhoe that they just took it for granted. I think that at times she thought she must be invisible sitting up there.

It is rather boring work once it becomes routine; your arms just automatically make the same moves over and over again. Everyone who has taken that job complained that it's hard to keep awake on the hoe. Barbara suggested a couple of times that she wouldn't mind learning to operate the gold concentrator, or jig, for a change, but the men decided she was doing such a good job where she was, why change? Later, she told them again that she would like to be spelled off for a while and work at something else, but they just smiled patronizingly and told her she was doing just fine.

About half an hour later, they heard the hoe shutting down. There must be a problem with it, they thought, and went over to investigate. Barbara was nowhere to be seen, and Rocky's pickup was missing. In about two minutes flat, Rocky was in Ted's truck and racing past the settling pond, through the trees, and over to their trailer.

He found Barbara, calmly throwing her sleeping bag and belongings into the back of the pickup. Rocky was stunned.

"What are you doing, for God's sake?"

"What does it look like?" she responded. "I'm going home."

"You can't do that—what'll we do for a hoe operator?"

She looked at him pityingly. "That's your problem. What you need to be concerned about is how you'll get your pickup back from Whitehorse. I'm leaving it at the airport."

Rocky had never seen this side of her before.

"Aw, come on Barb, don't do this, we need you—I mean, I need you. You can run the jig or anything else you want. Hell, you can stay home all day and read books—just don't leave... please."

Finally she gave in and began unpacking. But never again did those men take that little lady for granted.

Ted had a jig the same as the one we used, and Barb finally had the chance to run it, whenever she needed a break from the backhoe.

Rocky always kept a batch of his own beer on the go. Sometimes if it was a pleasant evening, we'd sit around the campfire for a while before going to bed, and Rocky would bring out a bottle of this homebrew for each of us. It was a special treat, not at all like the kind you buy.

Recreation

This was the year we bought three Honda "Big Red" three-wheel motorbikes, one each for Gordon and me, and a smaller version for Arkell.

I worried that he was a little young for a motorcycle, being not quite four years old, but his grandfather just scoffed at that idea. In fact, he was handling it like a professional in no time at all, but, being a little daredevil, he was going much too fast. Gordon had to tape the throttle down to slow him down. He couldn't figure out why the change all of a sudden.

"It's broken, Grandpa," he said.

"No, it's not," Gordon told him. "Maybe if you push harder on the handles it'll speed up a bit. But it's dangerous to go too fast, you know."

"Well, Grandma does," he replied.

After that we'd see him trucking down the trail in his little boots and helmet, pushing for all he was worth on the handlebars.

"Come on, go faster," he'd say.

Before long he was going everywhere with us when we took the bikes out, and the three of us took lots of mountain rides together.

Bear Cub

One night all the dogs in camp went crazy. Between one and two o'clock in the morning, they barked and raised such a fuss that we couldn't sleep. Grumpily, we blamed it on our visitors who had come out for the weekend; they had brought their two

198

huskies along, and *they* must have upset the resident dogs. They had settled down by morning, but around ten o'clock Naomi happened to glance outside. She saw the reason for the ruckus of the night before: a grizzly cub was up a tree, not thirty feet from our trailer. Evidently the dogs were used to him being there by this time, but he did not feel the same about them. He was hanging on for dear life.

A mother bear looking for her offspring was something we did not need around the kids in camp, and when one of the men suggested we shoot the cub, he met with the wrath of most everyone there.

Almost everyone was in camp that day, having decided to take a Sunday off for a change. We held a conference, and decided we'd bring all the dogs inside and disappear into our trailers with them, to stay very quiet and let nature take its course. In a few minutes it was so peaceful outside you could hear a pin drop. The whisky-jacks came around, and you could listen to the water in the creek running. All was still, the way I like it.

We were all watching from our windows, and after a while the bear very cautiously started to inch its way down the tree, stopping every few seconds to look around. Whenever he heard a slight sound, he would bound back up again. It must have taken him half an hour to get his hind feet on the ground, and even then he didn't want to let go of the tree. It looked as if he'd waited all night to urinate, because he left quite a puddle there. When he was finished, he bounded away, swinging his head from side to side.

I guess his mother must have found him because, later that day, Ron came across two sets of bear tracks in the mud not too far from camp, one large pair of paws and one small.

We didn't go back to Mount Freegold the next year; the paydirt on the claims we had been working was starting to thin out, so Kirk and Gordon spent the summer of 1985 doing exploration work and testing various creeks in different locations around the Yukon.

We moved around a lot that year, ending up back at our property in Atlin. We had kept the claims in good standing, and there were still some spots left that looked interesting.

Ted had acquired several promising mining properties, mostly hardrock, and had formed a public exploration company to develop them, which he ran from his office in Vancouver. He came up from time to time to organize drilling and work programs. By now he had quite a lot of experience in the mining field.

Kirk and Gordon didn't participate in this endeavor at the time, preferring to keep our operation a private joint venture as we'd always done.

17

The Klondike Goldfields

There was a property on Gold Bottom Creek, twenty miles or so out of Dawson, that Gordon had had his eye on for quite a while. Gold Bottom runs into Hunker Creek. A lot of gold had been taken out of the area during the gold rush. The old-timers, though, had always left a fair amount behind and, as methods and equipment became more efficient, the same ground was gone over several times—and proved to be profitable each time.

Barry Rouleau owned the leases that interested us, but rumor had it the price he was asking was totally unreasonable. Rather than take this at face value, we decided to ask Barry outright what he had in mind. But first, Gordon and I went in to the site to check it out. The seven-mile stretch of road from Hunker Creek was in pretty bad shape from recent rains; we jolted and bumped along over potholes, slid from side to side, and in and out of deep ruts in the slimy mud. Then we came to a large hole, and not knowing just how deep the water was in the middle, we thought we'd better get out and walk the rest of the way to avoid getting stuck. Picking our way over the high spots, we soon came around a bend and into a lovely, grassy clearing above the road with a green, forty-foot trailer and some outer buildings scattered around the perimeter.

There was a pair of black rubber boots on the porch steps, so we knew someone was there. As we approached, the door opened and Barry came out in his sock feet. He invited us in. Never before had I seen a mining trailer like that one. It was spotlessly clean, from the airy yellow curtains at the windows to the white linoleum tile on the floor.

We introduced ourselves. Barry told us his wife and kids hadn't arrived yet from Victoria, but as soon as school was out, they'd be along; unless, of course, he had sold the property by then. His wife, he said, was not in favor of selling it at all, but he was ready to try something different now. Then he took us on a tour of the property, giving us a rundown on what he had done and what his plans were if he stayed on. Barry did not have the lease on the property his trailer was on; or on the creek right across from it. They were owned by a man who was mining on Quartz Creek; he had told Barry he could use the location for as long as he wanted it. The Rouleau family had tended it with loving care for the years they'd been there, even building a greenhouse and growing a garden. Barry said he saw no reason why the owner of the lease would change his mind about letting someone else use the location for living quarters; and I thought how enjoyable it would be there if we ended up buying Barry's mining claims.

Barry's mining area started a quarter mile from his trailer, went down the hill, across a small creek, then up an incline a mile to the forks where Soap Creek ran into Gold Bottom. He held fourteen claims altogether.

Kirk came out with us next time we went to Dawson, and Barry went over the claims again with him. Both Kirk and Gordon could see a lot of potential there, and they didn't find the price too unrealistic. The only catch was that Barry wanted all his equipment to go with the deal, and we didn't really need it.

He was very firm on that point, however, and in the end the men decided they would negotiate the deal and sell what they could of the equipment.

On July 3, 1986, we signed an agreement for the fourteen claims plus equipment, at a cost of $145,000, in the lawyer's office in Whitehorse, and promptly moved out to Gold Bottom. We were still mining there in the summer of 1992.

Unfortunately, we had to move from our pleasant little grassy location the second year we were there. The miner who held the lease on Gold Bottom across from the site suddenly took a new interest in the property and sent one of his employees to work the claim. The fellow decided he'd need all the space for his own trailers and as a parking spot for equipment. So we hooked onto the green trailer—it had no wheels, just skids—and dragged it across the creek, up the hill, and onto a spot on our own property which we had cleared for it. It also meant putting in a long pipeline for our water supply, and relocating a lot of things—all just at our busiest time. It was a big disappointment to me, and even though the owner of that lease was entitled to the location, some of the pleasure had gone out of the mining life for me.

Eventually we bought a large portable water tank, which we located on the hill above the trailer, and pumped water into that from the creek. That gave us a steady water supply, and plenty of gravity pressure for the flush toilet. The bunkhouse down the hill had its own built-in water tank. So we now had water for the showers and the washing machine. Kirk hauled in another house trailer, as well, so we had plenty of accommodation.

The claims at the lower end of Gold Bottom Creek, at the Hunker Creek junction, were owned by a family by the name of Miller. Mr. Miller and his two sons were mining the property, and had been for several years before we came. One mile farther up the creek lived Ole Lunde and his wife Mary, also miners; another two miles brought you to Chris Weinert's camp, our young neighbor who was now living on the spot that used to hold the green trailer Gordon and Kirk had bought from Barry. And of, course, just across the creek from him now, was our outfit. Some friends of ours, Pete Erickson and his wife Margaret, were mining on Soap Creek, a mile above us at the forks.

As the mining season was so short, and we were so busy, there wasn't a lot of time to get acquainted with the neighbors. If we even got up to see our good friends Pete and Margaret, it was a rare occasion. We did get to see the other miners briefly sometimes, mostly from the window of our pickup. On a trip back to the mine from Dawson City, for instance, the first ones to come into view as we started up Gold Bottom Creek were the Millers, who were usually hard at work mining their land; a mile on up the road, we would wave at old Ole Lunde, digging away with his Cat or loader. Ole was a big man, who always wore a trucker's cap and overalls. Both his hands were gnarled into fists from arthritis, but he didn't let that stop him from running his Cat. Quite often we'd stop to pass the time of day with his wife, Mary, who would be hanging out clothes on the line, or sometimes just out walking along the road. Mary was in her late seventies then, a small, wiry, and spirited Scotswoman. She stopped us one day to give us some cranberry muffins she had made.

"You're looking well, Mary," I said to her.

"Well," she replied, "I've been exercising. Doctor says it will keep me young. Twenty minutes after every meal I go for a half-hour hike. Yes, I finally smartened up. First fifteen years here I had my face to the ground and my ass in the air all day, seven days a week. No more!"

Just before we reached home, we would pass Chris Weinert's trailers, and, if it was before noon, he and a couple of his crew would be lolling on the steps of the porch enjoying a bottle of beer in the sunshine.

"Is his outfit broken down?" I asked Gordon once.

"No, they just haven't got started yet for the day. They'll put in a good ten hours yet today before they quit."

Sure enough, most nights we'd hear the erratic roaring of the Cat's motor until almost midnight.

Chris always reminded me of a quick-draw cowboy you would see in an old western movie. He had long, sandy hair, tight lips, cold gray eyes, and a deadpan expression. A beat-up old miner's cap and ragged form-fitting blue jeans completed the picture.

It never ceased to amaze me that there was no holster holding a revolver on his hip. He had the lithe movements of a panther, swinging effortlessly up onto his Cat, much like a cowboy would swing into a saddle. 'A real tough hombre,' I thought to myself.

We always hoped we wouldn't meet Chris in his jeep on the narrow road to the mine, as he drove as if he were going to a fire.

Mining in the Dawson area, or anywhere else in the Yukon for that matter, is strictly a summertime occupation, as everything is frozen solid in the winter. Usually the ground can be worked from the first of June until the middle of October in a good year, and even then most miners have to contend with permafrost in the Dawson district, as it varies in depth in different locations. On our ground sometimes, on a north slope, the permafrost would be right under the moss on the surface, and then the big ripper on the D-9 Cat would come into its own. We would hit bedrock about twenty feet down.

The first old-timers who came along had to thaw the ground with bonfires before they could start mining. They'd take off a foot or two of overburden at a time until they reached the pay dirt, which was usually just above bedrock.

Later, giant dredges were built by the large mining companies to dig for gold, and they thawed the ground ahead of them with steam-boilers, driving in pipes as they went along. The dredges left row after row of long, uniform tailing piles snaking across the country for many miles, a sight plainly visible even today, especially from the air. Eventually, the whole Klondike valley was dug up this way. The dredges worked for over sixty years in the Dawson area.

A lot of smaller creeks, such as Gold Bottom, were not mined by dredges.

Flood

The water situation at our mine was always a source of worry. There would either be too much water or not nearly enough. A couple of rainy days could bring on a flash flood, washing down the whole length of the creek and taking out dams and settling ponds, and anything else that happened to be in the way.

When Pete, who worked above us, sensed that this was about to happen, he would jump into his pickup and speed down to warn everyone to get their stuff out of the way. Sometimes Pete got there in time, sometimes not.

There were times, too, when the dam that held the water in some miner's settling pond broke—this was usually caused by rain, too—and the muddy water would come rushing down the creek just like a flash flood, only dirtier, taking out the sluicebox of the unfortunate fellow below him, or maybe just loading it up with all kinds of mud and debris.

Relations could become strained at times like these.

A person never knew when it was going to happen to him, though, so it paid to be tolerant if you could find it in your heart somewhere.

It wasn't on Gold Bottom alone where this happened, of course; it was quite common in other areas, too.

I'll always remember the first time it happened to us. The rain had come just when we didn't need it. For three straight days. It didn't let up at all.

Kirk wanted to finish up the pit they were working in before moving the trommel to a new piece of ground, so the men were putting in full days in spite of the rain. The stretch of road to the mine was disintegrating rapidly. Every day the potholes were becoming deeper and sloppier, and the pickups were all the same color now—muddy. The strain was beginning to show in the faces and dispositions of the men when they came back to the trailer to eat. You could hear it as they kicked off their muddy boots in the back porch and struggled out of wet slickers and coveralls before coming into the kitchen for a hot meal. There were no jokes and no easy banter at the table. The men were as gloomy as the weather.

"Well, I'll tell you guys what we're going to do," Kirk told them. "We're all going to take some time off, until this weather clears up. This is for the bloody ducks! If you want to go into Dawson for a break, it's okay by me."

Our two helpers decided to go into town for the rest of the day, have some drinks in the bar, and come back the same evening.

"We'll hit her again tomorrow morning," Larry said.

I was in the trailer reading a book after breakfast the next day when I heard an unfamiliar sound. It was almost like thunder in the distance, but too long and steady to be that. Louder and louder came the roar, and I dashed outside to see what was happening. Suddenly it came into view, this torrent of muddy water rushing downhill past the trailer, filling the little creek and overflowing its banks along the way. Hot in pursuit came Kirk in his pickup, not even stopping to glance at me standing there in the yard; he was just burning down the road for all he was worth to warn Ole.

It was too late for Chris Weinert, if he had any equipment working in the creek, but Kirk should make it to Ole's in time.

As it turned out, Chris and his crew were away that afternoon, and Ole, fortunately, had nothing in the creek that the water could hurt. He appreciated being warned about it, though.

Kirk slept late the next morning, as he had been up until all hours the night before repairing the dam. Just after the other men had gone to work, Chris roared up the trail on his motorcycle, slammed on his breaks, and came to a stop just outside our trailer. He pounded on the door and, before I could answer, he had snatched it open.

"Where's Kirk?" he demanded.

Startled out of my wits, I pointed and said, "He's just over there, sleeping—"

Before the words were out of my mouth, Chris was striding down the little hill which led to Kirk's trailer. He flung the door open and went inside.

"Get up, you son-of-a-bitch," I heard him say before the door closed.

'Oh my god,' I thought, 'He'll kill him!' Not wanting to interfere, but still frightened, I paced the floor, trying to convince myself that Chris had met his match if he started pushing Kirk around. Dimly, I could still hear shouting and curses coming from both of them, even at that distance, and it was reassuring to know that both of them were still alive, at least. After a while things calmed down. They were in there for a long time, and I was just wondering if I should dig out the first-aid kit and go over there when the door opened—and out came Kirk and Chris, each with a bottle of beer in his hand, laughing hilariously and slapping each other on the back.

'Men!' I thought. 'Who can figure them out?'

Chris had got back from town just before he had come over, and found his sluicebox plugged with mud, logs, and debris of all sorts, just when he was about to start his day's sluicing. Figuring that Kirk had taken advantage of his absence to let the water go from our settling pond, he had seen red and come right over to have it out.

They had apparently settled the misunderstanding. Chris hadn't been mining on Gold Bottom long enough to know the whole score on the water situation there yet, either.

This episode became one of tales told around the gambling tables by the local miners in Diamond Tooth Gerty's on Saturday nights in Dawson. Everyone thought it was funny. I came to realize that our neighbor wasn't really the tough hombre I had imagined.

There was nothing funny about the water shortage, though, when it didn't rain for weeks on end. The creek would dry up to a trickle, and there were a few times when we actually had to shut down, as you cannot operate a trommel without water. The boys got quite expert at devising ways to build their dams for holding the water when it was plentiful. You had to be a good dam builder (damn good!) to survive.

The water was recycled again and again in a dry period, until it was too thick to use, and then the men would move the trommel and build another pond. Every day we would scan the sky for a rain cloud, hoping that when the rain did come it would last just long enough and not too long.

Gladys and Charles

Don't ever let anyone tell you the life of a miner is an easy one. Sometimes I think we must have been crazy. Then I think, 'yes, but it certainly wasn't boring, was it?' After all, how many people can sweep their kitchen floors every day as Gunn and I did after an afternoon of cleaning, and then have to pan the sweepings because there are little pieces of gold showing through the dust?

In the winter of 1986, my school chum Gladys and I renewed our friendship. She and Charles had lived in Spokane, Washington, ever since their marriage in 1943. Gordon and I went to see them and it was like all those years since we'd seen each other had never happened. After spending many hours reminiscing, we all agreed that they should bring their truck and trailer up north and spend the following summer with us at Gold Bottom. Actually, they ended up spending the better part of the next three summers with us at the mine.

Charles enjoyed hiking up the creek every day, trying out his luck with the gold pan. Gladys, Gunn, and I always managed to squeeze in a couple of hours in the afternoon for a game of Scrabble, or Tile Rummy, and most evenings Charles and Gladys would volunteer to do a cleanup for us at the jig.

It certainly lightened the workload for us. Gladys kept the best organized and most well-equipped trailer I have ever seen. It did not matter what we ran out of or needed, Gladys would slip over to their trailer and find it. She even brought along her mix master, and never seemed to run out of carrot cake. Where she kept everything is still a mystery to me.

The jig was the best investment we'd ever made for the mine, in my mind. It certainly made our life easier, almost entirely eliminating all the panning we women did in the past. In the Atlin days, we used to sit just outside the trailer for hours, bent over a big galvanized tub and taking turns panning all the buckets of concentrates from the sluice. When it became too cold or the mosquitoes were bad, we'd take the tub inside and do our work in the kitchen. Now we just emptied the heavy buckets into the jig and let it do the work. It was like a miniature sluicebox set up at waist level, with a vibrating bottom in it. About three inches of little round steel pellets, or ball bearings, were placed inside the box, and the concentrates were poured into a trough at the upper end to be washed through and over the ball bearings. Little by little, the vibration and water would move the material along the length of the box. The person operating the jig would help it along by gently brushing the top inch or two of sand and gravel on through, and removing the larger rocks by hand, eventually sending the tailings out over the end and onto a little ramp that was lined with artificial turf to catch any fine gold that might have escaped with the tailings. The jig operator would have to wear thick, waterproof gloves, as the water was very cold. This was a rather delicate procedure, as you had to use just the right amount of pressure, and resist the temptation to sweep it all down the box quickly just to get the job over with. During this process, while the little steel balls were jumping around, vibrating like mad, the gold particles would drop to the bottom of the box and into two funnel-like hoppers that were built onto the underside of the jig. These funnels had levers on them which we would pull from time to time during the operation to open the funnels and let the gold run out into a bucket. We usually set the jig beside a creek so we'd have lots of clean water, and place the small pump we used for this purpose right in the creek.

The road from our camp to Dawson City had to go through this shallow creek, right alongside the usual spot for the jig setup. Often while we'd be working there, people would drive by, most of them just sightseeing. Many of them stopped to see what we were doing. Those who had never seen a gold-mining operation would be quite impressed, especially if we were at the stage where there were a couple of pans sitting around on the ground with clean gold in them.

"Man!" they'd say. "Where are you going to spend all your money?"

"Well, after we've paid the crew and put a new set of running gear on the D-9, I think I'll take her to McDonald's for dinner next time we're in town," Gordon would joke.

Sometimes there was more than a grain of truth in that statement, too.

Then, looking up at the snow on the mountains one day, Gordon would remark, "Looks to me like termination dust up there on the hill. Guess it's time we were heading south for the winter."

Mining is much like farming, I think; you have your good years and your bad ones, and it really is the lifestyle that keeps most of us coming back year after year, moreso than the profits.

I always say that miners put all their money back into the ground (buying new equipment, for example) every fall, just so they can have the pleasure of digging it all up again next spring.

Island Home

In the winter of 1986–87 Gordon and I spent some time in our motorhome exploring Vancouver Island, and I fell in love with it. I was ready for a change of scenery and, I have to admit, a little easier lifestyle now. There was something about the sea and the surf, the boat marinas and the salt air that was new and inviting to me after living in the Yukon all my life.

"You have seen it before—when we've traveled this way," Gordon said, mystified.

"I know, but I've never thought of the possibility of actually living here. I'm really seeing it for the first time. The trees here

210

are so huge and luxurious, compared to ours. The Yukon is just as beautiful in its own way, but I would like to enjoy this atmosphere, too. We can still go back up north for the mining season."

I was ecstatic when Gordon agreed to the idea, and within a few weeks we had sold our home in Whitehorse, by phone, bought a new one in Saltair, and embarked on a totally different lifestyle, one more time.

When April rolled around, though, Gordon was champing at the bit to get back to what he calls the good life, and I found myself back in the mining camp on Gold Bottom, waiting for the busy season to begin.

I really look forward to the fall, when we go back to our new home; but I have never really regretted the day that Gordon said to me, "Why not try gold mining?" and I answered, "Why not?"

Epilogue

Jimmy Kane

Our neighbor Jimmy Kane was born at what is now Dalton Post long before the arrival in the area of the white man. In 1974, our son-in-law Cal Waddington taped a conversation with Jimmy about what his life was like at that time. Cal was kind enough to give me a copy for the purpose of including excerpts in this book. The following paragraphs are some quotes from the tape.

Cal's bridging passages are in italics.

Dalton Post still exists just off the Haines Highway at Mile 106, on the banks of the Tatsenshini River. When Jimmy was born there, Jack Dalton was unknown, and the village was called Nesket-aheen. Through Jimmy, I was able to reach back first-hand to the history of a pre-Dalton Trail.

JIMMY: That's our trail first—before Jack Dalton. Coast Indian. He pack in gun—stuff like that, you know—and we buy. We use that trail, that's our foot trail. Jack Dalton first white man go through, that's why we call him Dalton Trail. The first white man. I see it my own eye. I was pretty good man then...not too good yet! (He chuckles.) That trail been there way before Jack Dalton, before MY time, too, anyways, because foot trail you can see wear right down. That before I born, and before my grandfather born too, 'cause they use that trail for years and years.

CAL: For trading?

JIMMY: Well...us people can move ourself to that Hootchi country too—there use to be village there before Dalton Post. We call that Nes-ket-a-heen—that Coast Indian name before white man. The time I know, just the Coast Indian. He bringem white man's stuff—powder, gun, gunpowder, muzzle loader, and shot...marble shell, something like that, you know. But they got no cap, tho', that days, you know. They got some flint. He hit trigger with that rock, and the spark come—he go into the powder. But pretty hard, he just slow burn, and you—you gotta aim alla time before you shoot, you know.

The inland village of Nesketaheen, where Jimmy was born, was an important one, before the white man. I asked Jimmy how many people might have lived there.

JIMMY: Quite a few. All the Indian in this country...lots of people, Indian, stay because it's only place we getta fish, you know, that salt water fish...they stay there. We don't trap 'em like this time. Because that time we don't work, we don't think. That days we don't know coffee—we don't know salt—we don't know nothing. Just plain soup, that's all—no salt...We just eat—well, that's way we were born, you know. Think salt it's good, alright. I don't use too much salt—just a little bit, just taste like, you know. Days before white man, we catch anything. Any animal in Yukon, you know, little gopher, too, summer time. We cut 'em and we dry 'em. We smoke 'em good. Fish—meat—we cure 'em good, then dry. We bundle up, mostly groundhog...you know that whistler...we go up the mountain there, get quite a few. We smoke him good, lots of smoke—he need that. Fat, too fat, you know. That's why we put him in good smudge. Then we dry. Wintertime, he come good. Soup, you know. We got no coffee those days, we got no tea...just soup. Rabbits, we boil the fresh rabbits, then we put ONE groundhog in. Oh, you oughta see that soup—just like milk, that soup there, and we drink it...every bit of it that soup. Oh GOOD!

CAL: Jimmy, how old are you now?

JIMMY: Well...I'm not quite sure my age. 1899 August, mounted policeman come. Then they try to get our age. But we don't know. They told (us), the mounted policeman, 'How old you are?' I'm pretty tall man, then. Well, 'I don't know,' I say, 'I don't know.' They ask my Dad, 'How old he is?' 'We don't know,' he say, 'We don't keep track.' Then my mother he asked. 'No, we don't know.' He says, 'Before white man he born, so we don't know.'

When Jack Dalton come—that time he see me I was that big, you know. I don't know how many inch tall that time he see me, first, that Jack Dalton. That time they measure me. They try to guess my age then, you know. Go backward. Ever since, now I keep track ever since...94, right today.

CAL: Ninety-four. So the way of life you had before the white man must have been a good way of life.

JIMMY: Why sure, before white man, you know.

CAL: Jimmy Kane—that's a white man's name.

JIMMY: Well, because my dad is name Joe Kane. You know, just like white man. That's why I take my dad's name...white man call my Dad that, Joe Kane.

CAL: Do you have an Indian name, too ?

JIMMY: Oh, Yeah ! We got each one of them Indian name. 'Chedawoo' is my name. Is one of them Indian name. You see? Is pretty hard.

CAL: Maybe that's why the white man called him Joe Kane. Too hard to write. In those old days, Jimmy, did the Wolf and the Crow live together in the village?

JIMMY: Oh yeah! we gotta be Crow and Wolf, married. Crow married to Wolf and Wolf he married to Crow. But these young people today—they don't know what they doing now, they change a whole lot now.

CAL: The Coast Indian and your people—they get along good?

JIMMY: Oh, us and people from coast, we stay together just like brother—brother. And sometime us people want to stay down Alaska, for winter. Oh, lots of good place there—lots of good friends. That's the place they eat berries—all kinds of berries.

The trading route was important to the Coast Indians, as well as to the inland Indian, and no doubt was the reason for the trail in the first place, probably centuries ago.

JIMMY: The Coast Indian he bring white man's stuff like that from Sitka. That's the place they first stole. You've hear about Sitka, Alaska—that's Russian trading post (Jimmy says Rooshun). That's the place Coast Indian, he go there with a sailboat, you know. Then they pack into this country here. Well, we buy all together, everything. We got enough, then we go somewhere and we sell it. We got lots of fur again for the summer. The Coast Indian come—we get lots of stuff—then we got enough, we go ourself too just like Coast Indian, you know. We sell the guns or something like that you know—we get more fur. We trade 'em, yeah.

CAL: I hear stories sometimes about slaves.

JIMMY: Well, my time—I see one, two slave in Dalton Post. Only get Alaska Indian slave, I think. Well it's pretty hard to tell you, but I'm gonna tell you tho'. Long time (ago) people they fight war just like you people do now, you know. By and by maybe one-two-three kids saved, then they take 'em for the slave.

CAL: And then they keep them all their life for slaves?

JIMMY: All their lives, sure. Just like brothers, you know—they feed 'em good, they eat good, sleep good.

CAL: So not slaves like we know.

JIMMY: No, no, no. (He laughs.) He just work...he just work.

It was no doubt the trading route that maintained the good relationships between the Chilkats and the inland Stick Indians, although these two peoples did, according to Jimmy Kane, raid other tribes for what we know (mistakenly, as Jimmy pointed out) as slaves. There were apparently no massacres between the Chilkats and the Sticks, but there were wars between these two groups and their own adversaries.

One such war, between the White River Indians and the group who lived in the Nesketaheen area, around the Tatsenshini River and Dezadeash Lake, was evidently caused through a series of misunderstandings. The war took place on the shores of Dezadeash Lake. It was the last such Indian conflict.

Jimmy Kane remembers the story as handed down to him by an elder of the tribe, while Jimmy was still a young man. It's a complex tale, and difficult to follow, but by listening carefully, a picture of intrigue, misunderstanding, slavery, and accident emerges, all of which seems to have been begun by the eternal triangle.

215

JIMMY: Pretty long story. These people from the Labarge country come up there, two of them. And he married Indian women up there, that from this Dalton Post Indian. Oh, they stay there maybe four or five years then go back to Labarge. He leave his wife there. By and by he never come—he never come—two years never come back. His wife he marry to somebody.

CAL: Married somebody else—

JIMMY: Yes. That's why they start that war, you know. That not our business, though, but somebody else you know—yeah. So they come back—that man he come back for his wife. By and by he take away his wife again from that somebody.

CAL: He tried to take his wife back?

JIMMY: Well—he take him back, all right. He put her the pack and they gonna move next morning. My god, that fellow there he got the gun, he look, he watch them. He wait...he wait...he wait...it just about broke daylight. Then he shoot everybody he knows in there. He shoot with that marble shell, you know. Well the first, that Wolf, he sleep (on) outside, his brother, he sleep side him, and that man and his wife sleep way back, you know. Well, that gun there he killed two men—that shot, shot you know. Then he run away. Two men he kill. Well, that's what start that trouble. That Dalton Post Indian he say, 'You kill our customer.' The White River Indian, you know, that's where we get our fur from—that stuff like that.

Then they go hunt rabbits, Burwash—you know that Duke meadow that place there? By golly, they shot the rabbits, you know. They got no snow yet, the froze ground though (the ground was frozen).

CAL: That's the Dalton Post Indians?

JIMMY: Dalton Post Indian, come through the Labarge, you know. Right through that willow. He shot that people by accident, you know. From shooting rabbits, that shot he go fly from there, that frozen ground you know. Man he shot him there...he dead there. That the other people you know—that fellow he kill White River Indian. That a big bunch, too, you know.

CAL: Killed him by accident?

JIMMY: Accident. Because thought that Dalton Post Indian boy he killed a people—he not do that, just accident, you know,

216

he shot the rabbit then that...some shot he fly from the frozen ground, you know, and man he shot him right through his chest. He dead. That's the way they start war now. Well...they take the three young girls there, you know. Well, the boys—you know young boys—and that's with his wife, you know. That bringem down a bad one. Well, the White River Indian, they think so those women...girls...they think they get them for slave. That mistake right there, you know. That's when they come war here—and that war come, he drop—oh, lots of camps, I dunno how many camp tho', each one of 'em just full. They kill 'em, kids and all!

CAL: What about the other people, did they have guns?

JIMMY: Why sure, they had gun. I tell you about that. Eventime (evening time) everybody play, you know, for the old people—they loaded that gun you know.

CAL: That's old muzzle loader.

JIMMY: Yeah, that muzzle loader. That eventime Indian come and they swarm, you know, right close to that camp. Then everybody run in the tent—they shoot 'em. But they don't drop one at all. Then they empty gun, they turn him back then they start to play again. Always pretty lucky that way, before. But those White River Indians you know.

CAL: They didn't load those guns up again.

JIMMY: Nothing! No chance to load the time they fighting, you know. Then they come back. Just one save. Just one save.

CAL: They killed them all but one?

JIMMY: Just but one. He save! That one there he run away and that skin he cover him. He hide himself. That's why he save, that's all.

CAL: Just because he hid under a skin—

JIMMY: Yeah, under skin.

CAL: Part of the Hume family.

JIMMY: Yeah, that's only one save. If that one get killed you don't see no Chuck Hume around here now...(He laughs.)

CAL: That fight down there, that war, that was the last one?

JIMMY: Last one. Last war, that Dezadeash.

With the coming of the white man, the Indians' way of life began to change, and the trails through the rugged mountains between coastal Alaska and the interior—so jealously guarded for hundreds of years—were about to see, for the very first time, the White Man. In the late 1800s, increased numbers of prospectors, explorers, and missionaries moved up the coast from Seattle and British Columbia, and that secret trail was soon discovered. In 1880, Edmond Bean learned of the route, and in 1881 a missionary named S. Hall Young, and Rev. Sheldon Jackson established what was known as Chilkat Mission, near the mouth of the Chilkat River, and what is now Haines, Alaska. Then in 1883, Lieutenant Frederich Schwatka made the first official exploration of the route crossing into the interior. In 1890, Frank Leslie's illustrated newspaper organized an exploration party over the Chilkat trail into the interior. One of the young scouts hired for that expedition was Jack Dalton.

The trail impressed Dalton as an easy route inland, so the following year he and E. J. Glave explored the route to the Indian village on the Tatsenshini river. That village is now known as Dalton Post. This all happened before the Klondike Gold Rush, in about 1893.

Jimmy Kane remembers Jack Dalton's first visit. During his story, Jimmy refers to Dalton as "alimol," meaning animal. Then he clarifies his remark by likening Dalton to the "Kushtika," which is a kind of spirit which takes the form of any of the coastal and inland animals, a kind of Indian bogeyman.

JIMMY: Well, yes, I see the first white man—down the Alsac River. In the spring time, you know, we gotta go down meet that fish coming from the salt water—we cut 'em, then dry too. We got a cache there. That's the place we first see Jack Dalton. Everybody cutting fish, 'Somebody come,' they say. 'Somebody come!' That Jack Dalton. That Indian, he guide him. They walk down—he gonna meet that fish too, you know.

I was kid that time, you know. Well, I good size though. We never see no white man before. Indian say, 'Some alimol he got me!' That white man he mean. Animal, you know. He thinks he just like the Kustika! Well—he no think so, he just tell that thing. He know he white man, you know. The first time I see—he got little face, you know—just about that much you see his face. They all got the mustache, you know (he laughs) and that his partner, too. All mustache and little face. Jack Dalton he talk Coast Indian. He talk to somebody there. Oh, they listen! He tell 'em he want to go down to Dry Bay. One of the Coast Indian, he got a dugout. He hire two, that dugout canoe, he gonna drift right down to Dry Bay, and my uncle, my father's brother, was with him. He tell that men there they gonna go tomorrow. I listen. 'What you want Chief?' he say. He talk too—Tlinget—that man.

'What you want you get pay? Cash or anything.' Well that old Indian say, 'Ca-hoot.' You know, that mean beads, just about that long beads. (Jimmy laughs hard.) He give. He satisfied for that.

CAL: What kind of guy was that Jack Dalton. Was he a nice man, or bad man?

JIMMY: Well, he was a GUN man. Everybody scared that. He's a coeboy, you know. His partner, he look like big shot, you know. He don't talk nothing. He got little face, though. (He laughs.) He always give me something. Candy—you know, he keep in his pocket that thing. He give me candy—oh gee, too sweet for me, I can't eat. 'You put you mouth,' he say. I put my mouth. Gee, too sweet! I spit him out. (He laughs.)

CAL: So this Dalton guy, he started out as a cowboy in the States, did he?

JIMMY: (Confidentially.) Yeah, coeboy. He's coeboy. I see his revolver.

CAL: Did you ever work for him?

JIMMY: I work for him, anyway. He like me, too, you know. Any time, he told me, any time you see the horse, bring 'im up in the morning to Dalton Post. That's what I do—like horse wrangler, you know.

CAL: Did your people have horses before Jack Dalton came in?

JIMMY: (Disgusted.) What place we gonna getta horse? No place. Except in '98. We see lots of horses—oh, LOTS of horses that Dalton Trail that time. Played out, too much pack—too much ride too, you know. He just let them go. If there's some Indian woman, he trade one moccasin for one horse. That was some pay, ah? Oh, they just let 'em go, you know.

CAL: Did Jack Dalton get along good with the Indians ?

JIMMY: Oh, get along fine, get along fine. He sell whisky there, too, I see that. No policeman that days. You know that policeman come? 1899 in August. I know good that time.

CAL: And when did Dalton come?

JIMMY: Oh, way ahead. Before '98, way before '98. He sell whisky too. Indian know no law, that days. American stuff, he sell to Yukon. That before '98.

So Dalton Post actually existed some years before the discovery of gold in Dawson City. Even so, it must have been quite an undertaking to convince prospective customers that cattle could indeed be driven that distance into the heart of the Klondike. Jimmy Kane was there and remembers how an enterprising businessman contrived to set himself up as keeper of a toll road to the Goldfields.

JIMMY: Well, Jack Dalton, he take a chance, you know. He got fifty cattle, and he start right through to that Dalton Trail. They think they gonna be all dead. Well, that Jack Dalton, he just try. He take 'em through, that fifty cattle, by god. He lost one—nothing...he got broken leg in there. He got load to Fort Selkirk. Then he put in the advertisement that they can go through. By god, he beat it too. You see cattle—boy! They go through to Dawson City. The biggest band I see, 500 cattle, one herd.

CAL: How many men would they have to have with them?

JIMMY: Well, I suppose that 500 cattle, quite a few. Night and day they watch there. Maybe four men he watched at night, you know. Too many, you know.

CAL: Five hundred cattle—one time?

JIMMY: One time I see down there—just one herd—500 quite a few. You see that big flat there—just this side Seventy-five Mile. They give him rest there. They feed on country, you know, that grass.

CAL: There's lots of feed for them ?

JIMMY: Oh, lots of feed for them. Days and days you see cattle, some 300—some 350. That's the biggest herd I see—500. You oughta see cattle that time! And they pay that Jack Dalton, they use that his trail. Dalton—he no mistake—he know just what he try, you know. He got 'em. He pretty good man, I should say.

Cattle. The largest traffic over the trail consisted of livestock. The trail also played an important part in the famous U.S. Reindeer Relief expedition. The food crisis in Dawson City in the winter of 1897–1898 prompted Congress to appropriate $200,000 for the purchase of the reindeer herd to ship north to the Yukon. Over 500 of these harnessed, trained animals were shipped from Norway, brought across the United States to Seattle by rail, then shipped to Haines. A long delay in Seattle caused the supply of reindeer lichen to be used up before the deer reached the mountain meadows, some sixty miles up the trail from Haines. This resulted in the loss of several of the animals.

According to reports, 114 of those reindeer reached Dawson nearly a year later, in January of 1899. The food crisis had ended, and the expedition ended up needing aid rather than Dawson City. Jimmy Kane remembers seeing the harnessed reindeer as they passed near Penex Post on the Dalton Trail in the fall of 1898.

JIMMY: That time we see him, me and my dad, in the fall time. But different Indian, too.

CAL: What did they look like, those reindeer? Did they pack them?

JIMMY: Well they got a little pack. White man—that's all he need. Just one white man, but the rest were that Indians, he kill lots of caribou, wild caribou. Get mixed up with that reindeer—they shot 'em. Well you know — got that woodland caribou here—big one. But what they got—reindeer—only a little thing! He got big head, though...he got big horn. They got little pack too. They got big rope they drag around.

CAL: Could you talk to the people with them?

JIMMY: Well, we can't talk — different people altogether. Big tall people—Indian. Me and my dad we see 'em Penex Post— that mountain there. By golly, we see that big bunch of tent there, you know. We go alongside—we hunt for caribou. 'My golly,' my dad said. He hear about it before that. 'Look that people,' he say. Oh gee, that reindeer. Lots! Some place trail they got little bit that caribou moss. But the mountain you see lots of caribou moss, though.

CAL: They had to travel high then. Did they have any wagons or sleighs or anything hooked on those reindeer?

JIMMY: [By] the time they get Haines, they got a sleigh, you know, just made like a boat. Each one of them he pull, each reindeer. He follow other ones. No trouble. I see that reindeer sleigh, one time, this side Rainy Hollow. That time the snow gone there. Big pile there, boy, big as this house. They left the sleigh there.

CAL: So they could travel then in the summertime.

JIMMY: Summertime he just leave sleigh. They got lots of grub—just one white man, boss.

CAL: You think those sleighs are still there?

JIMMY: Oh yeah, maybe rotten tho'. Long time ago—long time ago.

CAL: Well, you and your dad actually went over and saw those people with their reindeer?

JIMMY: Yeah, then me and my dad we go and we see that people. 'That the people,' he told me. Well, I like to see it too, myself. Is big, tall people. And they cook—they cook like a fire roast, caribou, front quarter, the whole big ribs. That's when it lunch time. That white man, he just eat little lunch, that's all—just tea. That Indian there, he just eat nothing but meat.

CAL: It's funny they should take reindeer; it's a funny thing to do isn't it?

JIMMY: Yeah, funny.

It was funny when they reached Dawson, that gold-fevered town that had seen so many strange events. It was said that when the remaining reindeer and their herders appeared in the hustle and bustle of downtown Dawson, they attracted almost no attention at all. Around the turn of the century, as the [Dalton] trail's importance diminished, and the business venture lagged, Dalton returned to the coast. Jimmy Kane remembers his last meeting with Jack Dalton.

JIMMY: Well, last time I see Jack Dalton, down Champagne. He's pretty old. He talk to me pretty good.

'Look at our trail,' he say, 'a-u-r-r [our] trail! It's all just covered in sand, there.' That's all—the last I see Jack Dalton.

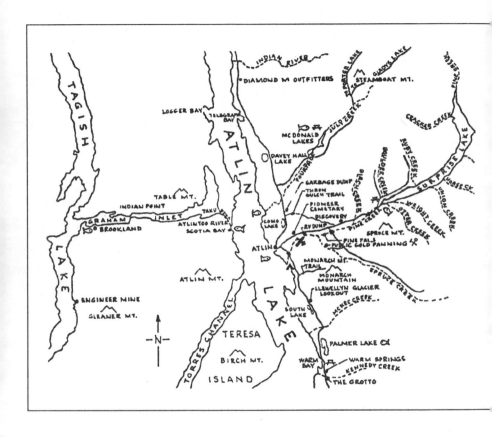